previous pages: *Corrupt File: 2012_0147*, 2013 (detail)
Colour inkjet print mounted on Dibond aluminium
200 x 156.2 x 7 cm

*Corrupt File: 2012_0157*, 2013
Colour inkjet print mounted on Dibond aluminium
200 x 156.2 x 7 cm

*Corrupt File: 2012_0147*, 2013
Colour inkjet mounted on Dibond aluminium
200 x 156.2 x 7 cm

# Contents

opposite: *The Second Hotel Vancouver*, 2014
Digital C-print mounted on Dibond aluminium
305 x 157 x 7 cm

***Hogan's Alley***, 2014
Digital C-print mounted on Dibond aluminium
157.5 x 309.9 x 7.6 cm

# And this you have forgotten?
# Fiona Bradley

'Memory is not a simple record
of events but a dynamic process
that always transforms what it
dredges up from its depths.'

Eric Hobsbawm[1]

Stan Douglas's *Corrupt Files* (pp.2–3, 5, 7, 151, 153–55) are startling. They do not look like his other work, and at first glance seem to have little to do with it. Large, rather beautiful, abstract images with variously clustering and separating stripes of purples, greens and yellows, their allegiance appears to lie more with the poured paintings of Morris Louis or Ian Davenport than the films and photographs of Stan Douglas. They don't look much like photographs, let alone Stan Douglas photographs.

They are, though. And as photographs, and particularly Stan Douglas photographs, they are what they are – no more and no less, and because no less then actually rather more. In Douglas's work conceptual possibilities tend always to be bound into material and technological actualities and the clue to these lies, as ever, in what they are and how they are made.

Each image has a direct relationship to one of Douglas's previous, representational photographic works and is the result of attempting to compress the digital data of that work for reproduction. It looks like the data has been scrambled, but in fact the data itself is not corrupt: this is what it looks like in the camera. It has rather not been *un*scrambled for easy interpretation by the human eye, or brain. To the camera, these beautiful streams of colour must be what the world really looks like. The works make any distinction between realism and abstraction somewhat pointless, similarly any residue of the old argument about whether or not a camera ever lies. The camera sees what it sees – the point is perhaps how we see (and understand) that.

The extraordinary photographs *Hogan's Alley* (pp.10–11) and *The Second Hotel Vancouver* (p.8) have a similar relationship to visual truth – one that is at once simple and mind-bendingly hard to understand. Although so detailed that as you look at them you feel almost physically drawn into them, the images in these

photographs are not photographs of real places, but are rather digital reconstructions, made from a great many old photographs, of what real places may have looked like in around 1948. The reconstruction process is complex and involves using a computer programme to apply photographic images (textures) to three-dimensional geometry (meshes). *The Second Hotel Vancouver* shows an Italian Renaissance-style building erected by the Canadian Pacific Railway in 1916, abandoned by the railway in 1939 and left derelict until it was squatted by homeless war veterans in 1946. *Hogan's Alley* shows a mixed black, Chinese and Italian neighbourhood, rife with bootlegging, gambling and prostitution. Both works are a kind of digital remembering – the computer constructing a complete present from a series of photographically remembered fragments of the past. Like the *Corrupt Files*, they present pure digital information, only they code it in a visual language we can more easily shape to look like reality.

All these photographs pull the past into the present, unearthing it, recoding it, restoring to view something previously repressed (in time if not in memory). The film *Der Sandmann* (the first work of Douglas's I ever saw and something of a touchstone for me, and many others, in approaching his work) is in all respects – materially, technologically, narratively, conceptually – precisely about that.

The film is set in a fictional Berlin *Schrebergarten*, or allotment, recreated on a film lot both as it is in the 'now' of the work (1995) and as it might have been twenty years previously. As the camera pans around in a complete circle, three people – Nathanael, Lothar and Klara – read letters they have written to each other. Only Nathanael is seen in person, and the narrative is his. He writes to Lothar of a recent return to his home city and the unease this return has engendered, centred an encounter with a strange old man. Lothar's reply reminds him that the strange old man is Herr Coppelius, who in their joint childhood imaginations they cast as the mythical and terrifying Sandman who puts out the eyes of children who resist sleep. The final letter, from Nathanael's sister Klara, links a daring nighttime expedition undertaken by Lothar and Nathanael to surprise Coppelius in his garden with the children being told of the sudden death of their father.

This narrative, and the words and letter format in which it is told, are taken from E.T.A. Hoffmann's 1816 story *Der Sandmann* which Freud drew on extensively

opposite and following images: installation views of **Der Sandmann**, 1995,
in 'The Oldest Possible Memory: Sammlung 1', Sammlung Hauser & Wirth, Lokremise St. Gallen, 2000.
Two channel 16mm film projection, black and white, sound, 9:50 mins (loop)

in *Der Unheimlich* (The Uncanny), his 1919 study of repression and anxiety focused around the phenomenon of the uncanny. Freud describes the uncanny, through an analysis of Hoffmann's story, as an amalgamation of different but linked affects. It is 'that class of the terrifying which leads back to something long known to us, once very familiar'; the constant recurring of similar situations; the sensation of finding yourself back somewhere you know you have been before. It is a 'repetition-compulsion'. It is a confounding of the self, 'through doubling, dividing and interchanging the self'. It is there where imagination and reality merge, so that 'an uncanny effect is often and easily produced by effacing the distinction between imagination and reality'.

Stan Douglas's *Der Sandmann* is an eerily beautiful, utterly compelling, multi-layered, virtuoso work which both takes from and adds to Hoffmann and Freud. The speaking voices tell the story of Nathanael's repressed memory of the death of his father and how the memory returns to haunt him in the 'overwhelming sense of dread' he feels on revisiting the places of his childhood. As ever with Stan Douglas, the work's technology reinforces its narrative, and the camera also tells the story – both the actual story, and the enmeshing of past and present, the remembered and the real it enacts. For as Nathanael is doubled, divided and interchangeable with the other speakers who share his narrative between them (his friend Lothar to whom he writes his appeal for clues to his sense of unease, his sister Klara to whom he mistakenly addresses it) the image on the screen is divided and doubled, moving from the present to the past and back again.

The film was shot twice. First, Douglas's camera panned a complete circle around the set of the allotment as it may have looked twenty years previously. Then it panned another circle on the exact same trajectory around the garden updated to 1995. The two takes were spliced together, duplicated and presented on a pair of projectors focused on the same screen. The projections are out of phase with each other by one complete rotation, and only half of each image is shown. The effect is that of a vertical seam down the middle of the screen, the right half of the image continually erased by the left in what Douglas calls a 'temporal wipe'.

As you watch it, the central seam between the two projections, at first barely discernible, moves towards Nathanael, speaking the text of his letter to Lothar: 'Dear Lothar, it's been ages since I've written…'. As the seam passes over his face, his lips drop out of synch, and things start to disappear, the 'old' garden replaced by

the 'new' one as Nathanael's present fears are articulated – 'it was as if I had seen it all before'. As Lothar takes over the narrative – 'how could you forget the Sandman?' – we see Coppelius pottering in his garden, erased by the present but then reappearing in it as his true identity is revealed by Lothar and his connection with 'the saddest moment of our childhood' is narrated by Klara. As the explanations subside, the camera returns to Nathanael, and he begins his story again, his lips this time dropping back into synch as the present is overtaken by the past for the second loop, which reinstates the 'old' garden in a circuit which, as you watch it, seems to overwhelm you with a visual sense of revelation and understanding: 'it was the Sandman!' (the film's final words).

Der Sandmann is a tale of repressed and restored memory, of selves doubled, divided and interchangeable, told in a doubled, divided and perpetually interchanging film loop. The mechanism matches the story, the two projectors becoming almost actors in the drama, playing out the tricks that memory can play. Two projectors, two projections, two versions of the same facts – in Nathanael's head and in front of our eyes. We see and we see, and we understand and we understand again, differently. How the work is made is an inextricable part of what it is, and what it is is inextricably linked to how it makes its meaning.

In this, Der Sandmann speaks clearly, if across a gap of almost twenty years (the period of time between the 'past' and the 'present' in Nathanael's narrative) to Helen Lawrence, the innovative play/film – filmed play and played film – whose first UK performances at the Edinburgh International Festival in August 2014 are the occasion for this publication, and for the exhibition at The Fruitmarket Gallery, Edinburgh it accompanies. The work is a classic noir drama, the genre chosen by Douglas for its close association with post-war reconstruction and self-reinvention: 'post-war periods are eras of normalisation when the criminality and black markets that thrive during war-time states of exception are no longer tolerated, even though the prior way of life is never completely forgotten [...] It was under these circumstances that the film noir style emerged in the 1940s, and the secrets jealously guarded by the tough guys and femme fatales of the genre are inevitably drawn from this period. [...] The urban fabric of virtually every major city in Europe and North America was radically reconfigured after the Second World War. [...] The setting for Helen Lawrence, Vancouver Canada circa 1948, is only one example of these changes among many but with its own peculiarities: governed by quaint morality laws that everyone knew everyone else ignored, and populated with a mix of British expatriates and other immigrants who wanted to forge new identities for themselves at the furthest edge of the western hemisphere'[2]. *Helen Lawrence* is acted on an almost empty stage. As well as acting, the actors also film each other acting, the footage synched in real time into a digitally rendered 'set' (this is where *Hogan's Alley* and *The Second Hotel Vancouver* come from, and in) and projected onto a screen between the actors and the audience. It's a work about mistaken identity and unstable memory, about reconstruction and reinvention and the long shadows the past cast into the present.

With its doubled and divided action, its twice absent set (much of the synched action 'takes place' in *Hogan's Alley* and *The Second Hotel Vancouver,* those digitally reconstructed no-man's-lands between photographs past and present[3]) and its hackneyed narrative, seemingly half remembered and certainly somewhat predictable from countless other *noir* plots, *Helen Lawrence* is, like all of Stan Douglas's work, a masterpiece of effaced distinctions. Between, as Freud would have it, reality and the imagination. And, to think again of Hobsbawm, between reality and memory. And even – to return to *Corrupt Files* for a moment – between reality and abstraction. The actors and the cameras all do what they do and see what they see. The point is, perhaps and again, what we make of that.

## REFERENCES

The title is a quotation from Lothar's letter to Nathanael in *Der Sandmann*.

1.   Eric Hobsbawm in conversation with Hans Ulrich Obrist. Quoted in Hans Ulrich Obrist, *Ways of Curating*, London, 2014, p.57.

2.   Stan Douglas, writing in a promotion document for *Helen Lawrence*.

3.   Details from the two photographs *Hogan's Alley* and *The Second Hotel Vancouver*, appear throughout this publication (pp.22–23, 48–49, 66–67, 148–49).

*Midcentury Studio: Suspect, 1950*, 2010
Digital fibre print mounted on Dibond aluminium
74.6 x 87.9 x 4.4 cm

*Midcentury Studio: Dice, 1950*, 2010
Digital fibre print mounted on Dibond aluminium
187 x 150.8 x 7 cm

*Midcentury Studio: Intrigue, 1948*, 2010
Digital fibre print mounted on Dibond aluminium
75.2 x 69.5 x 4.4 cm

*Midcentury Studio: Cache, 1948*, 2010
Digital fibre print mounted on Dibond aluminium
75.2 x 86.7 x 4.4 cm

# X Marks the Spot
## Simon Baker

———————

'Accidents and Crimes…Each day
the city promised me them afresh and
when evening came it was still in my debt …
A looted display window, the house from
which a dead person had been removed,
the place on a carriageway where a horse had
collapsed – I would plant myself in front of
them to feed on the evanescent breath left
behind by the event…'

Walter Benjamin, *Berlin Childhood Circa 1900*[1]

Anonymous, **Mine Town Blaze**, 1960

The incidents, accidents and crimes that Walter Benjamin found just out of reach, writing in 1932 seem, in retrospect, entirely photographic. This, after all, was the man who had likened Eugène Atget's photographs of the streets of Paris to the scenes of crimes, before adding 'is not every square inch of our cities the scene of a crime? Every passer-by a culprit?'[2] The scene of a crime, however, for Benjamin, was necessarily deserted, bereft of incident or content, and photographed after the fact 'for the purposes of establishing evidence'.[3] And in his *Berlin Childhood*, Benjamin's obsessive drive to 'see' the city, to have it reveal its accidents and crimes, seems always doomed to failure, the needling of an insatiable desire. 'Even if a fire should still be burning,' he wrote, 'you would not see anything. It was as if the city, having taken jealous care of the rare flame, nurturing it deep in courtyard or attic, envied anyone a glimpse of the glorious incandescent fowl it had raised there for itself...'[4]

If, for Benjamin, the incident, accident, or crime, was always somewhere beyond the periphery of available vision, this reflects or relates to his interest in photographs which were emptied of action and consequently more provocative for the imagination, more properly marvelous in the surrealist sense of the word; 'the eruption of contradiction within the real'.[5] The photograph, in these terms, drawing on what Benjamin would coin the 'optical unconscious', had the capacity, as he put it, to 'pump the aura out of reality like water from a sinking ship'.[6] But while this held true for Atget's 'crime scenes' and the uses to which they were put, there is an inherent contradiction in thinking through this kind of image in relation to the 'accidents and crimes' of *Berlin Childhood*. It is difficult, for example, to imagine Benjamin responding in the same way to real images of accidents, or the crime-scene photography of the time. No-holds-barred, blood and guts exposés like *X Marks the Spot: Chicago Gang Wars in Pictures*, a gruesome, and heavily populated (by dead bodies at least) account of the murderous events surrounding the St Valentines Day Massacre in 1929.[7] This brutal and visceral book, illustrated primarily by photographs taken before the corpses of its principal subjects were replaced by Xs for official publication, found a home elsewhere at the time, reproduced and discussed by Georges Bataille in the dissident surrealist magazine *Documents*, just as Benjamin was thinking about Atget.[8]

Such photographs, by their very character, refuse to submit to unconscious projection, returning the viewer over and over again to an obsessive dead end with their own relentless and terminal logic that is, nevertheless, equally, and fundamentally photographic. Akin to what Bataille theorized in *Documents* at the

Tony Lombardo, King of the Mafia, and a lieutenant for Alphonse Capone. (Left) Madison and Dearborn Streets where Lombardo was assassinated one summer afternoon.

Anonymous, detail from **X Marks the Spot: Chicago Gang Wars in Pictures**, 1930

time as 'non-transpositional' images, which demonstrate only their own powerlessness and can only ever function in a rhetorical way.[9] They suggest, with a whole category of photographic material, that it might be possible to consider the logic of Benjamin's argument reversed: rather than worrying about photographs starting to resemble crime scenes (whether in a surrealist sense or Benjaminian one), what happens if the scenes of crimes become exemplary photographs? Which is to say, what is it about the language of the *mise-en-scène* that adapts itself to photography's rhetoric, language and grammar?

There is something striking in any (historic or contemporary) reappraisal of vernacular, commercial and press photographs, which suggests that they are somehow more honest; less forced and contrived. Such projects, which rely on the rhetorical susceptibility of their contents, can be traced back at least as far as the 1920s. But they are also everywhere today, following in the wake of conceptual projects like Larry Sultan and Mike Mandel's 1977 masterpiece of photographic appropriation, *Evidence*.[10] From the reclaimed everyday poetry of Luciano Rigolini's stunning sequence of vernacular images *What you see* (2008), to the ongoing publications of the Archive of Modern Conflict, that, like David Thomson's *82* (2013), offer new time and space to forgotten and overlooked photographs. Such rehabilitative projects, however, nevertheless reiterate the insignificance (or lack of apparent 'value') of entire classes of image rendered abject by the conventional histories of photography prioritized by museums and theorists.[11]

Like the images from which these contemporary publications were compiled, historic commercial or journalistic 'snapshots', taken quickly (often with synchronized flash) for newspapers in the analogue age, seem, somehow, to sidestep neurotic doubts about the artfulness and formal manipulation of the work of more sophisticated (and somehow therefore less authentic or honest) photographers. And even when they are evidently 'tampered with', their pre-reprographic interventions (white-out paint and retouching) seem boldly and frankly declared on the surfaces of the originals: marks of pride, rather than shame.

Stan Douglas has written of the automatic, or automatist nature of midcentury press photography, citing Weegee in America and Ray Munro in Canada. This same automatism is, he says, 'one of the primary arguments against photography being regarded as a legitimate art form' and is precisely what the photographs that make up his own *Midcentury Studio* 'espouse as an idiom'.[12] And yet, it goes without saying, although they may appear to speak the same language, this is precisely what Douglas's photographs are not. Posited as the cumulative work of a notional midcentury contemporary of Weegee and Munro, 'who was introduced to his craft during the war and [who] tried to make it into a business in the post-war period', everything about *Midcentury Studio* (like every aspect of almost every work Douglas has ever made) is determined and controlled to the last degree.[13] It is in the space

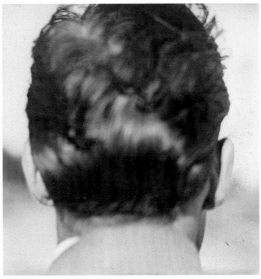

Luciano Rigolini, *What you see*, 2008, pp.66–67
Anonymous photographs

between the notion of the 'automatic photographer' and the staged scene that *Midcentury Studio* responds to Benjamin's impossible desire to see, and fix forever, the incidents, accidents and crimes promised but never delivered by the city of his childhood.

**Henry Wessel,** *Incidents No. 5*, 2013
Silver gelatin print on paper

To open up this space, and understand what it means to attempt to
restage the vernacular event, to work between the automatism of the midcentury
studio photographer and the precise performative choreography of Douglas's work,
it is worth thinking through their relative rhetorical structures with reference to two
contradictory modes of photographic practice. On the one hand the American
photographer Henry Wessel's series *Incidents*, published in 2013, but drawn from
work from the 1960s onwards, and on the other Cindy Sherman's better known,

*Untitled Film Stills*, produced in the late 1970s.[14] In the Venn diagram of overlapping pictorial and rhetorical concerns, both share different qualities with Douglas's *Midcentury Studio*.

Wessel's *Incidents* consist of 27 photographs selected from the entirety of his back-catalogue of material, which seemed to him to be transformed somehow by the framing notion of the everyday event or 'incident'. There is no attempt in *Incidents* to make a coherent narrative but the images are sequenced deliberately as a series of discrete examples that offer the viewer a fly on the wall (or fly in the sky) account of the way that Wessel sees the world around him. In Wessel's California, as in Benjamin's childhood Berlin, the everyday world is full of significant moments that are always on the verge of being overlooked and vanishing into oblivion. Evidently however, these dramatic scenes that Wessel 'finds' everywhere are produced through the combination of his skills at observation and the mechanical speed and acuity of the camera; many (especially those taken through car windows) existing only for the split second that the shutter opened. Furthermore, the sense in which they 'become' *Incidents* is entirely rhetorical, their character established by their proximity to their neighbours in a sequenced series. As such *Incidents* joins other Wessel series like *Odd Photos* in that they reveal both Wessel's practice as a producer and consumer of his own work; which is to say that while he never set out to photograph 'incidents', or 'odd photos' as such, he did find, in retrospect, that that was what he had been doing.[15] This, it has to be said, is far from the automatism that Stan Douglas identifies in midcentury commercial photography, but it does conform to the definition of the value of photography credited to Wessel's great friend Lee Friedlander, which goes along the lines of 'you take a picture of one thing and you get all this other stuff you didn't notice as well...'

For Wessel, the found 'incident' is something at odds with, or running perpendicular to, his original intention, but which nevertheless has the capacity to support a kind of rhetorical projection: these everyday factual scenes of the lives of others achieve a peculiarly dramatic fictional quality under the auspices of their re-presentation. They are appropriated scenes in almost exactly the terms that Duchamp defined the ready-made: an 'ordinary article of life' for which he had 'created a new thought'.[16] This correspondence is doubly striking in the context of Wessel's work, which seems somehow to open up questions about staged photography by evoking Duchampian nominalism: there are composed scenes and 'film stills' everywhere, he seems to say, you just have to look.

Sherman's *Untitled Film Stills* are probably too well known to need detailed explanation or discussion here, but suffice to say that they draw their power and effectiveness from perfectly simulating the look of stills from movies that don't exist, with the uncanny caveat that over the series as a whole, all the characters in each 'still' are in fact the same actress (Sherman). They direct us to draw conclusions from painstakingly produced artificial prompts, the clichés and conventions of various forms of midcentury B-movie and *film noir*. As such, engaging with the language of cinema, each single image proposes a longer narrative from which it seems to have been cut, but which, at the same time, it explicitly refuses. We know there is no 'moment before' or 'moment after' a Sherman film still, but the withheld potential is everywhere nevertheless. By contrast, with Wessel, we know full well that each incident is snatched from a real life narrative of which it was a single moment (however inconsequential), but that its characterization as 'incident' suggests an abundance of more consequential and dramatic imaginary alternatives. In essence, while Sherman uses the conventions of film to produce a still image that remains at a standstill, Wessel uses the conventions of photography to suggest the appearance of narrative cinematic effects.

In this context it is impossible not to think of Stan Douglas as an artist working between the conventions, technical capacities and medium-specific qualities of both still photography and the cinematic image, as well as between fact and fiction. And returning to *Midcentury Studio* it seems increasingly likely that there is something deeply significant about the scene or 'incident' transposed from one visual language to another, but wherein both languages remain, somehow, operational. In the original idiom of the midcentury studios that Douglas used as the basis for his work, photography is used (always carefully captioned), as proof of an event or scene. Equally important, however, is its technological capacity to capture movement or detail (split-second events, hard-to-see phenomena like textures or flames), and its evidentiary capacity to establish the identity of a person or place (like the images contained in *X Marks the Spot*…). Whereas, by contrast, in the photographs from Douglas's *Midcentury Studio*, the constructed scene is used to offer proof of the efficacy and qualities of the photographic medium to posit these same things in general: its ability to capture movement, detail and drama, and to suggest the components from which scenes and identities are established.

And, at the same time, Douglas is also concerned with another of the specific qualities of the photographic medium that is sometimes overlooked: its inherent

**Cindy Sherman**, *Untitled Film Still #48*, 1979
Silver gelatin print on paper

reproducibility. For what marks out the press photograph from the fine art photograph is that as a result of its rhetorical destination, to exist in relation to text in a mass circulation format, all midcentury press photographs are necessarily 'pre-reprographic': that is to say that they are only 'completed' as images after their final reproduction. Douglas's *Demobilization Suit, 1945* (p.42) gestures precisely to

of the photograph as both reproduction and 'to-be-reproduced', it is precisely *like* (but definitively *not*) thousands of press photographs heavily retouched with white-out for a reprographic process within which this intervention would (eventually) be entirely invisible. Either by the low grade of half-tone printing, which would eliminate signs of additional brushwork, or (as in this case, presumably) by cropping around the white-out. Playing both with scale and with the quality of the photographic image, Douglas transforms its nature and rhetorical potential while remaining deep within the original idiom of the midcentury press photo. There is a sense then, in which the images that make up *Midcentury Studio* are not only themselves 'arrested' scenes and actions, but that as images they have been constructed only to be extracted from the normal flow of their reprographic and rhetorical destinies.

This dramatizing of the characteristics not only of what Douglas calls the 'idiom' of the press photograph, but of the process of production and use, is all part of the performative side of a complex self-reflexive practice. For in *Midcentury Studio* Douglas re-stages the conditions under which photographs are produced and consumed, specifically to put into question the rhetorical and contingent nature of the image, both on its own terms and as part of a series. Indeed, the varying degrees of diversity and coherence in the photographs that comprise *Midcentury Studio* is itself significant: each work is dated to suggest where in the trajectory of the post-war career of the hypothetical studio photographer the works are supposed to have been made. In 1945 there is *Demobilization Suit*; while in 1947 there is a short series apparently dealing with side-show tricks and the suspension of disbelief; *Flame* (p.45), *Smoke* and *Rings*; and then the years 1948–1950 see the darker, criminal world of *Cache* (p.31), *Burlap* (p.134), *Incident* (p.46) and *Suspect* (p.25).

In each case, however, the specific idiom with which Douglas engages demonstrates the innate capacity of photography to stage the evidentiary function of the photograph. Works like *Flame* and *Incident* are demonstrative of the ways in which photography openly declares its potential for accuracy and reliability, but also of the ways that, within this idiom at least, any such photograph, unmoored from its original context, begins to reveal a secondary rhetorical function. Instead of denoting 'this happened' or 'this is real' they begin instead to suggest merely 'this are the kinds

opposite: **Midcentury Studio: Demobilization Suit, 1945**, 2010
Acrylic on digital fibre print mounted on Dibond aluminium
149.9 x 121.9 x 5.1 cm

of things that cameras can record and this is what they might look like if they had been photographed'. This, in a way, is why there is so much at stake for *Midcentury Studio* in historic precedents like Sultan and Mandel's *Evidence*, more recent vernacular projects like Rigolini's *What you see*, and Henry Wessel's *Incidents*. For in each of these 'real' series, the photographs included struggle to perform the tasks for which they were originally produced, and begin to do something else, to perform a secondary rhetorical function. Indeed, Benjamin points to this potential in vernacular photography when he suggests that 'a snapshot does not simply render more precise what in any case was visible, though unclear: it reveals entirely new structural formations of the subject.'[17]

In Douglas's *Midcentury Studio*, however, the 'original' function of the image is itself a fiction: they are planned, staged and executed only to resemble, in the most abstract way, the kinds of photographs that have real tasks and evidentiary functions. And this, perhaps, is why the notion of the *mise-en-scène* is so important, pointing, as it does, to the intersection (or overlapping) of fact and fiction in the operation of the photographic medium. The complexity of Douglas's work, however, is far greater than that of simply staging an absence of fact while pointing to this process, for it also reveals a technical sophistication, and an interest in the technical capacities of the photographic medium, that completely transcends the automatic-press-photo idiom with which they engage only to depart. *Midcentury Studio* is, it has to be said, a series of fantastically complex directed performances and technical propositions, partially disguised as casual snapshots, but which, on closer inspection, reveal themselves for what they are. While on the page, for example, they might seem closer to their 'authentic' forebears, in the gallery, their large scales and production quality (including strangely over-sized mount-board) gives the game away. Indeed, it seems in places, (*Cricket Pitch, 1951*, for example), as though Douglas has produced scenes to be photographed, of intricate arrested motions, that should only ever have been possible 'automatically', the first time round. This fascination and mastery of complexity sets Douglas's work at odds with the vernacular simplicity of the source material whose idiom it nevertheless continues to share, and brings *Midcentury Studio* into line with his recent practice in film and new-media. *Hogan's Alley* (pp.10–11), which exists as a 'still photograph' in only the

opposite: ***Midcentury Studio: Flame, 1947***, 2010
Digital fibre print mounted on Dibond aluminium
90.5 x 72.1 x 4.4 cm

most superficial sense, is in fact a virtual stage set constructed for the performances of real actors. This hugely complex and minutely detailed fiction takes this notion of staging a scene, or to be more specific, staging the idea of a stage, to a kind of conclusion. For here is a complete fantasy bearing all the hallmarks of a second order of fiction, the film or theatrical set, which, in its intended final form, will become the virtual space within which real actors perform the drama of his play/film *Helen Lawrence*. In *Hogan's Alley*, finally, Douglas has produced a scene that only looks like a photograph, and every square inch of which, as Benjamin suggested, promises incidents, accidents and crimes.

## REFERENCES

1.  Walter Benjamin, *Berlin Childhood Circa 1900*, trans. C. Skoggard, Jank Editions, Portland, OR, 2010, p.89.
2.  Walter Benjamin, 'The Work of Art in the Age of Mechanical Reproduction', in *Illuminations*, trans. H. Zohn, Schocken Books, New York, 1960, pp.219–20.
3.  Ibid.
4.  Benjamin, *Berlin Childhood*, op. cit., p.93.
5.  Louis Aragon, *Paris Peasant*, trans. S. Watson Taylor, Exact Change, Boston, MA, 1994, p.204.
6.  Walter Benjamin, 'Little History of Photography', in *One Way Street and Other Writings*, trans. E. Jephcott & K. Shorter, Verso, London & New York, p.218.
7.  *X Marks the Spot: Chicago Gang Wars in Pictures*, The Spot Publishing Company, Rockford, IL, 1930.
8.  Georges Bataille, 'X Marks the Spot', in *Documents 7*, 1930, pp.437–38.
9.  Georges Bataille, 'The Modern Spirit and the Play of Transpositions', in *Documents 8*, 1930, pp.48–52; trans. M. Richardson & K. Fijalkowski, in Dawn Ades & Simon Baker, *Undercover Surrealism: Georges Bataille and Documents*, Hayward Gallery, London, 2006, pp.240–43.
10. Larry Sultan and Mike Mandel, *Evidence* (1977), DAP, New York, 2003.
11. Luciano Rigolini, *What you see*, Lars Muller Publishers, Baden, 2008; David Thomson (ed.), *82* (vols. 1 & 2), Archive of Modern Conflict, London 2013.
12. Stan Douglas, *Midcentury Studio*, Ludion, Antwerp, pp.6–7.
13. Ibid.
14. Henry Wessel, *Incidents*, Steidl, Gottingen, 2013.
15. Henry Wessel, *Odd Photos*, Steidl, Gottingen, 2006.
16. Marcel Duchamp, 'The Richard Mutt Case', in *The Blind Man*, New York, 1917.
17. Benjamin, 'The Work of Art...' op. cit., p.230.

opposite: ***Midcentury Studio: Incident, 1949***, 2010
Digital fibre print mounted on Dibond aluminium
186.7 x 150.8 x 7 cm

*Malabar People: Cab Driver, 1951*, 2011
Digital fibre print mounted on Dibond aluminium
104.1 x 78.7 x 5.1 cm

*Malabar People: Longshoreman, 1951*, 2011
Digital fibre print mounted on Dibond aluminium
104.1 x 78.7 x 5.1 cm

*Malabar People: Student, 1951*, 2011
Digital fibre print mounted on Dibond aluminium
104.1 x 78.7 x 5.1 cm

*Malabar People: West-Side Lady, 1951*, 2011
Digital fibre print mounted on Dibond aluminium
104.1 x 78.7 x 5.1 cm

*Malabar People: Dancer, 1951*, 2011
Digital fibre print mounted on Dibond aluminium
104.1 x 78.7 x 5.1 cm

*Malabar People: Female Impersonator, 1951*, 2011
Digital fibre print mounted on Dibond aluminium
104.1 x 78.7 x 5.1 cm

*Malabar People: Owner/Bartender, 1951*, 2011
Digital fibre print mounted on Dibond aluminium
104.1 x 78.7 x 5.1 cm

*Malabar People: Waitress I, 1951*, 2011
Digital fibre print mounted on Dibond aluminium
104.1 x 78.7 x 5.1 cm

# Time On Show: Heterochrony in the work of Stan Douglas

## Mieke Bal

---

'A historical drama is staged in fragments, encouraging viewers to imagine a more comprehensive situation'.

Stan Douglas[1]

'Yeah, you never know when it's gonna back up and bite you. Give the kid a break.'
Percy Walker/Wallace in *Helen Lawrence*[2]


## Introduction: What is a Subject?

Stan Douglas is an artist I admire enormously. But I don't know him. I prefer it that way. I believe the life of art depends on the (metaphorical only) death of its author, and that the task of the critic is to look hard at the art and give a vision of it to the public; not to do the artist's bidding. Douglas does not appear much in the media. So, whoever is curious about him is best off looking at his images. Some of which are portraits. The 2011 series *Malabar People* (pp.50–65), for example. Is there a contradiction between his media-avoidance and making portraits? I will argue there is not.[3]

This artist who is a master of media and constantly combines old and new, declines to be a media star. This reluctance fits well with the concept of the subject he has so convincingly analysed in Samuel Beckett's late plays. As quoted in an interview with Scott Watson, Douglas learned from Beckett 'the doubt, that pronounal doubt, doubt of pronouns, doubt of the certainty of an *I*, [that] is the *a priori* of my work. And it's a doubt which is understood by people who are outside of the dominant representation.' The crucial importance of such doubt for an art that binds the artistic to the social becomes clearer in a 1988 catalogue essay Douglas wrote for an exhibition of Beckett's teleplays he curated: '... Beckett admits that the limits of his culture are not the limits of possibility .... The difference in Beckett [from the Sadean libertine] is that in place of this closed world (which has been invented in order to be mastered) he imagines

1. Wall text for *Luanda-Kinshasa*, video, 2013 in the exhibition *Mise en Scène*, Haus der Kunst, Munich, 2014.

2. Dialogue in *Helen Lawrence* written by Chris Haddock. The extensive catalogue for the exhibition at the Haus der Kunst, Munich, contains the full script of *Helen Lawrence*, pp.166–85. *Stan Douglas: Mise en Scène*, León Krempel (ed.), Prestel, Munich, London, New York, 2014 (quote on p.168).

3. Douglas's anti-heroic stance can be seen as an endorsement of the 'death of the author' thesis. On this idea, see Roland Barthes's 1967 essay 'The Death of the Author,' in *The Rustle of Language*, trans. Richard Howard, Hill and Wang, New York, 1986, pp.49–55. I consider this 'death' metaphor as a device to encourage better, more active looking at art, not to discount the importance of the artist.

Production photographs from *Helen Lawrence*, 2014
Chief James Muldoon and Percy Walker/Wallace

an uncertain one: the residence of an even less certain subjectivity.'[4]

The subject Stan Douglas is, for me, an artist engaged with time on behalf of the present. That is where 'he' is, and where 'I' am, and where history is happening. Along the lines of my earlier reflections on the bond between art and the political, I consider his work profoundly political – because, not in spite of, the fact that it is not *about* politics. What I mean by that will become clear in the course of this essay. His media: the media; his tools: research, narrative, suspense, the imagination, and history.

In Douglas's work, there are many signals of the refusal of an individualistic sense of identity. Many of his photographs and stills from his videos demonstrate this. What we have, then, is his art: films and photographs rather than paintings in a particular 'hand'. And now, a film/play of a form he has invented, about a white woman in the 1940s, *Helen Lawrence*. Nothing is personal. There are no autobiographical revelations, nor is there any anecdotal knowledge about him distracting us from the complexity of his works. And yet, the work can be recognized as his. For its incredible subtlety rather than any form of self-expression; for its passionate commitment to the importance of history in the present. For the way he uses formal perfection to pay homage to people kept from visibility. For the way he turns 'preposterous history' social. His project: the visualization of 'heterochrony,' the experience of the heterogeneity of time. There lies the political force of his work.[5]

In spite of an insistent anti-individualism, Douglas has made an entire series of photographs that can be considered portraits: *Malabar People* (2011). Yet, historically as well as generically, the portrait is the genre of individualism par excellence. As such it was class-bound; only the worthy citizens, mostly the rich and powerful, deserved to have their portrait painted. But his portraits are not individualistic at all. Like August Sander's famous *People of the Twentieth Century*, Douglas's *Malabar People* are mostly titled after their professions. Frontal, half-body, posed

4. The interview with Scott Watson was published as 'Vancouver Artist Stan Douglas Excavated the Ruins of the Past in Search of New Utopias', *Canadian Art,* Winter 1994. Douglas's text on Beckett (1988) was reprinted as 'Goodbye Pork-Pie Hat' in Scott Watson (ed.), *Stan Douglas*, Phaidon Press, London, 1998, pp.92–99.

5. I have developed the concept of preposterous history in *Quoting Caravaggio: Contemporary Art, Preposterous History*, University of Chicago Press, Chicago, IL, 1999; and that of heterochrony in the context of 'migratory culture' in Mieke Bal and Miguel Á. Hernández-Navarro, *2MOVE: Video, Art, Migration*, Cendeac, Murcia, 2008 (exh. cat.), pp.13–80. On political art as not about, but performing the political, see my trilogy *Endless Andness: The Politics of Abstraction According to Ann Veronica Janssens*, Bloomsbury, London 2013; *Thinking in Film: The Politics of Video Installation According to Eija-Liisa Ahtila,*

portraits, the sitters looking the viewer squarely in the eye: these are individuals but the works consider them in relation to society, beginning with their direct addressee, the viewer. This is one of the many paradoxes of Douglas's art. When I say 'paradox' I mean this emphatically in the sense of an apparent contradiction only; one that activates more complex looking so as to understand why this is, precisely, *not* a contradiction. Paradox is, in this sense, the best weapon against binary opposition and the severity towards contradiction adhering to it; a figure of infinite enrichment, serving a multiplication of possibilities.[6]

Take this clown: enigmatic, hidden, the clown gives access only to his outward aspect, just like an artist who shuns self-exposure. The traditional wide grin of the clown is clearly painted on, and we are familiar with the image of the fundamentally sad clown from other depictions, among which the sources that Douglas has used. *Clown, 1946* (p.77) is part of *Midcentury Studio*, a 2010 series of large photographs that '… chronicle[s] the burgeoning discipline of press photography in North America during the post-war period. Douglas has assumed the role of a fictional, anonymous photographer to create a series of images hypothetically produced between 1945 and 1951. To do so, he constructed a veritable "midcentury studio" using authentic equipment as well as actors to produce carefully staged, black-and-white photographs that painstakingly emulate the period's obsession with drama, "caught-in-the-moment" crime-scenes, curious and exotic artefacts, magicians, fashion, dance, gambling, and technology.'[7]

The artist's interest in the period immediately after World War II is consistent, and continues with the new film/play *Helen Lawrence* (2014). But his probing of historical time is not limited to a binary temporality between the 1940s and today. Instead, he creates *dense time*. This incorporates the late nineteenth century, the 1930s, the 1940s–early 1950s, the 1970s, and today – all historically decisive short periods, bound together by hope and failure, as well as periods during which

Bloomsbury, London, 2013 and *Of What One Cannot Speak: Doris Salcedo's Political Art*, University of Chicago Press, Chicago, IL, 2010.

6. See George Baker's decisive article on Sander's portraits: 'Photography Between Narrativity and Stasis: August Sander, Degeneration, and the Decay of the Portrait', *October* 76, Spring, 1996, pp.73–113. Much of Baker's analysis can be brought to bear on Douglas's *Malabar People*. In this connection, Fiona Tan's installation of video portraits, *Countenance* (2002), offers the other flank, so to speak, of Douglas's portraits.

7. This is drawn from the press release of the David Zwirner Gallery, New York. See Stan Douglas, Christopher Phillips, and Pablo Sigg, *Stan Douglas: Midcentury Studio*, Tommy Simoens (ed.), Ludion, Antwerp, 2011. Please refer to this book for any images from this series not illustrated here.

Mary Jackson and Buddy Black

the development of media made unheard-of leaps. Moments, also, 'when something significant seemed to hang in the balance'.[8]

This historical spread over certain key periods of modernity is most clearly presented in *Crowds and Riots* (2008), a series of four photographs which are (fictionally) dated 1912, 1935, 1955, and 1971 respectively. In the series *Midcentury Studio* to which *Clown, 1946* belongs, the dates range from 1945 to 1951 over the difficult recovery period after World War II during which press photography began to thrive. Another series of eight staged photographs, *Disco Angola* (2012), juxtaposes two scenes – the development of disco as a short-lived free-place of music and sex in New York and the decolonisation war in Angola – both from the mid-1970s. In all these works, a strong bond appears between social history and media history. This will turn out crucial for our understanding of Douglas's work.

In spite of, or against our cliché image of the sad clown, here, the clown's eyes do not betray sadness – a psychic *state* – but rather the brief *moment* of utter concentration of someone practising a difficult trick. Hence, the restriction to outward visibility subtly includes a more hidden, more difficult, and potentially disturbing aspect: an awareness of permanent danger and the constant need – from one instant to the next – to make the utmost effort to stay on top of the danger. Only an artist of Douglas's calibre is able to show this, as well as, at the same time, the miracle of the temporality involved.

The clown's two hands are clutched around two oranges. So, how can a third orange be in the air, without the blur that normally betrays movement in still photography of action? Is it defying gravity? When we look closer, we can find two tiny signs.

The clown's right eye (on our left) looks at the second orange, making the clown cross-eyed; and the thumb of his left hand (on our right) stands up, hinting at the opening of the hand to catch the next orange in its fall, but also pointing at the orange still in the air. This thumb is slightly blurred, as is the orange it holds. The first orange, in the clown's right hand is also slightly blurred albeit less so, suggesting a time line that leaves the third orange, the one in the air, paradoxically as the only one that is gloriously sharp, its pitted skin entirely readable. These are the only details that betray actual movement of the body in time. The sharpness of the orange in the air partakes of the magic that quite a few of these photographs have as their topic, and that obliquely also comments on the media miracle. These kinds of signs bind the still

8. David Campany, 'The Angel of History in the Age of the Internet', in Krempel, op. cit., pp.12–17.

*Midcentury Studio: Clown, 1946*, 2010
Digital fibre print mounted on Dibond aluminium
151.1 x 121.9 x 5.1 cm

photography to the videos in Douglas's oeuvre, by means of an incipient narrative quality, or *narrativity*.

Once these signs accede to our awareness, it becomes a very complex image. The gleaming clothes become a hindrance for the clown's dexterity, as we can see in the knees straining against the fabric. The hair standing up now hints at fright. Whatever you make of it, from this moment on, one of Douglas's typical mini-stories emerges. What he did in his 1991 series of mini-films, *Monodramas*, has here been condensed in a single still photograph. Once narrativity is set in motion as the viewer is sensitized to the subtlety of the details, however, nothing further is offered; no resolution, not even a plot, or intrigue (to allude to one of the other images in the series, see p.29). Below I will develop the idea that narratives without plot are means of activating viewers to experience temporality, and this is how Douglas turns still images into moving ones. It is, then, not a coincidence that he makes still photographs as well as films and videos; nor that he affiliates himself to Samuel Beckett.

His images speak for him – not for his life and emotions, but for what he has to say, in a fundamentally dialogic mode of visual communication. In time and in media, no work of Douglas's is single-layered. In *Helen Lawrence* this becomes an explicit formal topic, what the artist calls a 'visual polyphony,' both demanding and exciting if we aim to understand the dialogue. The images have a lot to say. The image of the clown is dated 1946 – the year of my birth and considerably earlier than the artist's birth – and then 2010. Time is invoked, and multiplied. The first date is fictional; the second real, or so it seems. My interest rests on this: how his art helps us look better, think better and perhaps, act better. This rather hyperbolic claim for art as it bonds with the political through a probing of the media and what they do, rests on the following aspects of Douglas's work: research, history, narrative (including suspense), fictionality – all in the interest of creating, with his viewers, a dense, heterochronic, experiential sense of time. In this essay, I will go through a few works to bring forward these aspects of Douglas's art. They help understand its importance as a reflection on time, with any subject there may be being subject to (his or her) time. In line with this speculative interpretation, this essay is subjective. It is *partial*, in two meanings of that word. It only deals with a few issues and not, by far, all the issues this rich body of art puts forward; and it is subjective, bound to my own interests. Inasmuch as I am subject to Douglas's work, his notion of (failed/risked/impossible) subjectivity colours mine to haunt it. This is the work of my imagination his images facilitate to fill in the gaps between the fragments he stages, as *per* the epigraph to this text.

## Researcher

The first aspect I want to look at is the connection between art and research. Douglas's publications often present the works first with a section titled: 'Historical background'. This speaks to me; I have always been a researcher, and only recently – some twelve years ago – I started to make art, 'become an artist'. This was not to entertain myself with a hobby, or to change my life in a desire for variation, but to push my research further. It was because I felt my writing was an insufficiently adequate medium to render the complexities I wished to present. The research I could do was neither solid nor subtle enough. During the process of making films I became more and more aware of how much I learned, both from the raw footage and from the editing; how making something that was visual art was infinitely richer qua knowledge than my academic documentation so far.[9]

Stan Douglas is an artist. But the way he makes his art is based on very serious, in-depth research – historical, literary, visual, sociological and technological. His images suggest as much. He is a man of many disciplines; that is the freedom of the artist, which he uses to come up with complex visions. In this sense, he is an 'intellectual' artist – but one who refuses to distinguish between cognitive and affective intelligence. I have artists like him in mind when I think art *is* research, a specific form of it, and in addition, can be based on (more) research. These are two different aspects of the processes involved. Only very few artists, and even fewer researchers, manage to integrate the two activities successfully. Douglas is one of them, and his success is due to his fundamental principle of art-making: *combining*.

This raises the question of time and history: why would he date his *Clown* with the year 1946? Dating artworks is a documentation issue, not an artistic one; unless it is done fictionally. I will return to the issue of fictionality and its knowledge-producing capacity. For now, I just mention the year as the one after the end of World War II, the slow beginning of rebuilding semi-destroyed societies, and the need and difficulty for war veterans to find work. It is Douglas's fiction. This, in turn, recalls that such veterans were in large part responsible for the golden age of photojournalism. Understanding this cultural emergence of press photography out of political tragedy and economic precariousness is part of the intellectual thrust of this work. A parallel suggests

9. To date, I have made experimental documentaries, video installations, and two feature fiction films. See www.miekebal.org/artworks/films.

Edward Banks and Julie/Joe Winters

itself with the convergence of the invention of cinema and the conquest of the American West.[10]

Through the simple act of his fictional dating, Douglas presents a thesis of a historiographic order, speculating on the bond between the history of photography and the horrors of war. And if we think for a moment of the traumatizing effect of war as experienced by soldiers – a reflection fragmentedly present in *Helen Lawrence* – the sense of imminent, although micrological danger in the photo of the clown becomes extremely poignant. A clown, in 1946 – how would that compare to a clown in 2010, the year the work was 'really' made? At the very least, the image establishes the task of the artist as a historian of visual culture. The meticulous reconstruction of the period style is thus a key element of the series' thrust. In line with my beginning on the absence of the artist and its anchoring in Beckett's plays, I also retain the clown as a *masked* subject. What lies behind the mask – hardship, trauma, melancholy, effort, futurality? *Helen Lawrence* hints at some partial answers. But the clown's mask needed to be established first, as a visualisation of the 'pronounal doubt' of the uncertain, unnameable subject mentioned above.

Douglas, as especially the images from *Midcentury Studio* in this publication demonstrate, goes deep into the documentation he finds to make his art. His research is not at all limited to finding stylistic precedents, although he has clearly researched the archive and thoroughly understands many formal principles. He researches both the social-historical situation of the subjects and the history of the medium. Recalling the early 'chronophotography' of Étienne-Jules Marey, Douglas's images of a dancer manage to combine – or, as the artist would say with a key term of his work, re-combine – the late nineteenth-century fascination with recording movement and the post-war interest in staging.[11]

The most striking detail, for example, in *Dancer II, 1950* (p.108), is not so much the whirlwind of the dancer's body multiplied in time – through the multiple exposure strobe light effect – but the simultaneous staging of a play, visible in the hands that break through the whirlwind.

10. On this convergence, see Nanna Verhoeff, *The West in Early Cinema: After the Beginning*, Amsterdam University Press, Amsterdam, 2006. Douglas's 1986 film installation *Overture* fits Verhoeff's analysis perfectly. On this work, see p.95.

11. On Marey, see François Dagognet, *Étienne-Jules Marey: La passion de la trace*, Hazan, Paris, 1987. For a positioning of Marey in the larger issue of capturing time, see Mary Ann Doane, 'Temporality, Storage, Legibility: Freud, Marey, and the Cinema', *Critical Inquiry* 22, Winter, 1996, pp.313–43. 'Recombination' is, as I will argue below, Douglas's special brand of fictionality.

12. Louis Kaplan, '*Midcentury Studio*: Entertaining Stan Douglas's Photographic Remakes and Double Takes', pp.19–41, in

In its companion piece, *Dancer I, 1950,* an incomprehensible hand in the bottom-right corner, easy to overlook, attracts the dancer's look. I see in this hand the conductor, in other words the artist, whose hand remains marginally visible, not to sign the work as his but to acknowledge responsibility for it. In terms of specific research, it has been advanced that these images are 'in direct dialogue with [Glon] Mili's stop motion portraits of the dancer Betty Bruce (1941).' This solid historical fact does not, however, account for the entire research endeavour Douglas is involved in here.[12]

The fact of this reference may be undisputable; but the point of it remains open to interpretation. This is where artistic and academic research may cross swords – or as I prefer it, join forces. Is it the boasting of possibility the artist references, the then-recently rediscovered capability of photography to capture movement in this way, or is it the socio-cultural ambience of gyrating choreography as both entertainment (culturally) and precarious living (socially)? Rather than answering this question by choosing either one of these options, I contend that the artistic research Douglas performs for and through these photographs pursues an understanding of how these two possible interpretations and many others hang together. His commitment to period style is not to represent it adequately, but to reconfigure what mattered in that time, so that we can see it is still with us.[13]

The series of sixteen portraits in *Midcentury Studio* called *Malabar People,* deploy this conception of history as heterochrony, while also addressing, or redressing the tradition of portraiture as a point of subjectivity put in doubt. Allegedly portraying people involved in a seedy nightclub at the edge of Chinatown, these images combine the frontal look and the empty (here, black) background of classical portraiture with a sombre, very un-classical vertical shadow that seems to divide the subjects into two halves. But no; these are not two but three sections if you count, as the images compel you to do, the dividing shadow not as line but as space. As Pablo Sigg sees them, these works 'document a society that has become dissociated from itself and the world where it exists'.[14]

*Stan Douglas: Entertainment,* Melanie O'Brian (ed.), pp.19–41, The Power Plant, Toronto, 2011, p.21.

13. Movement in photography had been an issue of intense interest in the late nineteenth and early twentieth century, as made famous by Eadweard Muybridge and Marey. Thus, Douglas's temporality in *Midcentury Studio* is already triple.

14. Pablo Sigg, 'A Gnostic Fable: Midcentury Studio', pp.22–31 in Douglas, *Midcentury Studio,* op. cit., p.29. On boundaries and borders as spaces for negotiation rather than dividing lines, see Inge E. Boer, *Uncertain Territories: Boundaries in Cultural Analysis,* Mieke Bal, Bregje van Eekelen and Patricia Spyer (eds), Rodopi, Amsterdam and New York, 2006.

Harry Mitchell and Betty Mansfield/Helen Lawrence

To the possible frustration of an academic historian, the actual historical environment remains hidden – it no longer exists. Three years later, however, with the photograph *Hogan's Alley* (pp.10–11) a photograph of one side of the 'set' of *Helen Lawrence*, we can get a displaced and retrospective sense of it. In the maze of half-crumbled houses, ruined wooden walls, sharp lights indicating inhabitation, and on the far left, the sign 'Canadian Junk ... Co Ltd.' we see the link to today. Ruins, and junk. At first I misread the lettering as 'Bank'. My partiality: banks seduce and cheat us, and junk is the result. The crumbling of capitalism. Yet people, we are led to think, live there, then and now, even though the neighbourhood recalled here was destroyed in 1972 – another of Douglas's focal periods. If the image, shot from high up in a bird's-eye view and made without a camera, presents us with a maze where no human body is in sight, it's because we get lost in there. The patches of light here and there structure the composition. This image retrospectively illuminates *Malabar People*.[15]

There certainly is a division inside these images that substantiates Sigg's view. But before jumping from the individual to the social aspects, and from art to documentation, it is worth considering how this transformation is negotiated. These portraits imply a profound understanding of the history of portraiture as a genre. Far from being a nostalgic invocation, however, these works radically undermine that genre's bond with class distinction. But they deconstruct it, rather than simply opposing and then reversing it. The people portrayed assert their displaced life as the ground that makes them worthy of portraying. They do this either by assertive gazes and defiant poses (*Dancer,* p.59: *Female Impersonator,* p.60), a certain endearing shyness (*Owner/Bartender,* p.63: *Waitress I;* p.64) or a subtle look of resignation (*Cab Driver,* p.51; *Longshoreman,* p.52).

The shyness of the sitters, so distinct from the proud people in traditional portraiture, is visible in that body part that, in posed photography, betrays the unease of models: the hands. Of the sixteen photographed people in this series, five have their hands hidden in their pockets, some have them behind their backs, one gives them purpose by clutching a wet cloth, and four have gloves on. Only the *Dancer* displays her hands clearly, but then, her entire pose is artificial; she is performing, not 'being'. She is also the only one who overtly smiles. These looks and poses, while indexing psychic states as social, also convey a more general resignation to being captured in the time document that is photography.

15. At the time of this writing the companion piece, *The Second Hotel Vancouver,* is still in production. I can only imagine what the contrast between the two places will add to each.

16. On the concept of allo-portraits, see my article 'Allo-Portraits', in *Mirror or Mask: Self-Representation in the Modern*

This involves the viewer, who cannot remain indifferent to these frontally-offered expressions. Because of the relationship between the genre and its undermining in these works, the people cannot be reduced to the individualism that traditionally inheres in the genre. This turns the images into 'allo-portraits' of sorts: portraits of individuals as something other than naked psychology; instead, like the hidden/failed/alert/moving subject of *Clown, 1946* (p.77), they are masked; their subjectivity in doubt. This visual theory of subjectivity as always (also) masked, then, is an unexpected gift from people divided and united in their severance from the mainstream society.[16]

Helen Lawrence, the eponymous character of Douglas's new film/play, can also be considered as masked. Dressed, coiffed and made up like the impeccable lady, she becomes the stereotypical femme fatale of *film noir*, and thus loses whatever individuality she might otherwise have had. In the opening scene before the credits, she is being administered electroshock which was, and again is psychiatry's way of masking the subject by destruction. A year later, when the play really begins, she takes the fake name of Betty Mansfield to avoid detection both by the police and by the ex-lover she is trying to locate, and who has also taken a fake name to avoid her. The name can also serve, not to identify but to mask, then. The name 'Helen Lawrence' is pronounced only once, at the end, once she has escaped Vancouver and is boarding the same train to the US as the ex-lover who is trying to escape from her revenge, deciding to do so by re-seducing her. Re-: the prefix sums up Douglas's philosophy of time as dense, circular, and re-cyclable.

For *Helen Lawrence*, Douglas again did meticulous research, in the files of the trial of a corrupt chief of police. No sentencing is recorded. The open-endedness in reality rivals that of the play. The entangled relationship between the aesthetic achievement and the commitment to the social domain that, in Douglas's complex temporality, is still with us because it comes from a past we have not been able to cut off is, in my view, the point of such meticulous historical research. And that research is subsequently turned into a fiction for a reason. Douglas does not simply continue a tradition; he inquires what the point of it was, and how this tradition was socially meaningful; and then, how it impacts on cultural uses of these technologies as they have evolved today. History lived, liveable or unliveable, today: this is his object of research.

Age (*Berliner Theaterwissenschaft* 11), David Blostein and Pia Kleber (eds), VISTAS Verlag, Berlin, 2003, pp.11–43. The term 'allo-portrait' was first used by Philippe Lacoue-Labarthe, quoted in Marianne Hirsch, *Family Frames: Photography, Narrative, and Postmemory*, Harvard University Press, Cambridge, MA, 1997, p.83.

Julie/Joe Winters and Harry Mitchell

## Historian

The second element of Douglas's work I am partial to is, thus, the commitment to history. This commitment prohibits a slavish adherence to history in a simple sense of a reconstructible linear past. Instead, the works demonstrate a desire to explore and show the complexity of history; its 'preposterous' refusal to stay in line; and the way it brings heterochrony to our experience of temporality. This complex is what the artist shows, or, in the way *Helen Lawrence* is designed, puts on show. Showing is the artist's method, and here he shows what it is to show, and to show time. But how can you show time itself?

This is one of the many reasons I see why *Helen Lawrence* is presented with a double-layered projection – and this in the double sense of that noun. On a stage bathed in blue light (recalling Derek Jarman's 1993 film *Blue* as the tool and setting for the imagination), practically empty (in reference to economic hardship after the war) but for a narrow bed that appears a few times (binding the asylum with the decrepit hotel), we see the actors play, in real time. We also see them film one another. 'In synch', but in fact, simultaneously with this live performance in colour, before it, a semi-transparent scrim shows the images they are shooting, now in black-and-white and from different angles immediately edited to show close-ups and the furniture and other period indexes that are lacking from the stage behind. Simultaneously, yet edited while they are being shot: it seems impossible, yet it is happening, both image strands in the same real time.[17]

The doubling of the moving image, one theatrical and one cinematic, shows what the media, then and now, are capable of, and how the past is needed to 'really' see the present. On one level, the transparency of the scrim means just that: transparency. But, traditionally used for the rhetoric of truth unencumbered by narrating subjectivity, here transparency becomes the tool to display that very subjectivity, impossible as it is, especially in the close-ups the double presentation allows, but also as the temporal interface. The endorsement of the past in the present also shows in a third layer, modest in size, crucial in importance: we can see the images on the LED screens of the video cameras the actors use to film one another. And when, at some point, one of the characters, the hotel manager Harry, dolls himself up to seduce a woman, he looks into a mirror when putting on a wig. But there is no mirror. Instead, he looks straight at the viewer,

17. On the material and symbolic meanings of the scrim, see Catherine Soussloff, 'To Begin with the Scrim', in Krempel, op.cit., pp.160–165, especially p.160.

18. Lacan's psychoanalytic theory of the

look on the projection. Straight, yet indirect, mediated by the old *film noir* aesthetic. Film is the mirror, then; and it is as indirect and hence, deceptive as the mirror is according to Lacan. This is the experience of time as multiple, not linear. It is an experience of time in the present that carries the past within it. Hence, it cannot be individual, even if it needs individuals who live it.[18]

*Helen Lawrence* has, at first sight, a somewhat simple *noir* plot, full of corruption, illegal gambling, prostitution, blackmail and theft. And although there is a constant threat of risk for all characters, there is no satisfying denouement. What matters, instead, is a sense of departure, of futurality, from beginning to end. At the beginning all the characters are at risk of losing what they have, especially their *place* – location and bread-winning – and they all explore what future they can escape to. They stand on the edge of the present as an abyss into which they could tumble. But they suffer from the fact that time is not linear. One historical backdrop that complicates the plot and exemplifies the refusal of time to stay in line is the traumatized state of returning war veterans. This is a tiny, understated but crucial motif in the work.

It is against the backdrop of trauma – to which I will return – that the futurality that is the red thread and only hope throughout the play is also set in a negative tone. At the end of the performance, two of the characters, Julie, the young orphaned daughter of a war victim who, trying out different identities, calls herself Joe, meets up with Rose, a Japanese woman turned up to take racist abuse and horny invasion by Perkins. He is one of the men in power, the likely murderer and future 'real' murderer. The two women arrive at the station just when Helen boards to join her former lover and traitor, Walker/Wallace. Rose, it turns out, caught as she is in her need for protection, money and love, feels dumped. Julie, who seemed to have a crush on Betty/Helen, feels something similar.

> Rose: We could go someplace else.
> Julie: We could go anywhere. Who's gonna stop us?

These are the play's final spoken words.

---

subject, while not referenced directly, is quite important in its backing of Douglas's Beckettian conception of subjectivity. For a lucid but not simplified exposition, see Kaja Silverman, *The Threshold of the Visible World*, Routledge, New York, 1996.

*Der Sandmann* (1995, pp.14, 17, 18, 21) divides time literally, again in a multi-layered view of time. The two-track projection has a visible seam in the middle. And although this line is extremely thin, after *Helen Lawrence* and *Malabar People* we are bound to see it also

Harry Mitchell and Percy Walker/Wallace

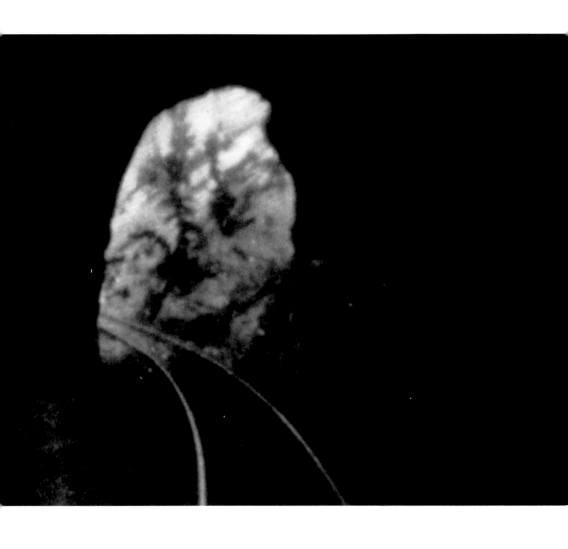

still of *Overture*, 1986
Single channel 16mm film projection
black and white, sound, 6 mins (loop)

as a space of negotiation. Sometimes the figure of the old man in the film disappears behind what only then looks like a screen. According to the work's soundtrack, a literary text read by three voices, this is Coppelius, or the imagined Sandman from E.T.A. Hoffmann's tale that inspired Freud to develop his theory of the equally complex temporality of 'the uncanny'. This visible seam in the middle of the work divides the garden, clearly studio-made, into before (1970s) and after (1990s) the reunification of Germany. Meanwhile, the 360-degree pan punctuates that divide spatially. If this line is thin, it may be read, retrospectively, as the relative failure to properly negotiate the (communist) past with the (capitalist) present, with the division remaining unproductively sharp as a consequence. The character of Nathanael, when he is reading his letters, disappears behind the screen that one half becomes in relation to the other. This becomes a three-dimensionality of layering in a two-dimensional, flat image.[19]

In this endeavour the artist goes farther than a doubling of time, however. To articulate how, I invoke one of his early cinematic works, *Overture*, from 1986 (p.94). There, he plots a triple (at least) history. The installation consists of a montage from the earliest days of cinema, the late 1890s, of silent footage shot by Edwin S. Porter for the Edison Film Company, owned by the developer of the movie camera and the phonograph, the machine for sound recording, as well as the light bulb – technologically, we are at the beginning of what Douglas's tools are today. Entering a narrow tunnel, skirting an abyss: the then-new railway appeals to fears of different kinds, in a tone that resonates with the gothic. The effect of such images is characteristic of what is called, with a felicitously ominous term, 'phantom rides'. A camera is mounted on a train, and while the train rides, we are close to experiencing the ride. This has become a metonymy, of the pars pro toto or synecdoche variant, for cinema. Today, Douglas makes this clear: in *Helen Lawrence,* significantly, the train as theme recurs, both at the beginning and at the end. At the beginning, right at the moment that the woman on stage is getting electroshock and thus seems the source of the scream we hear, the theatre play transforms into film as the scream turns out to be that of the train's whistle. The train races by in various positions and compositions. Travel through space, but caught in a capitalist endeavour that thrived on the new slavery of, particularly but not exclusively, Asian workers brought in for the purpose, is a recurring motif in Douglas's work with time. In *Helen Lawrence,* the shots are experimenting with, but not exactly doing the phantom ride. The book-ending of the story by trains riding, however, fulfils a function for the fictional play similar to the phantom ride,

19. See the analysis of this work by Fiona Bradley in this volume, p.15ff.

Sergeant Leonard Perkins and Henry/Hank Williams

namely of locking us up inside train travel as time travel.

For *Overture*, it matters that in the phantom ride, we as spectators *inhabit* the situation of the passengers. For future reference, let's retain the term 'phantom ride' and remember to link it to the currently hot topic of the spectre, and keep in mind that 'inhabiting a situation' is one of the key terms in Douglas's art. A situation, however, that the viewer is in charge of completing, on the basis of the fragments offered by the art – see the epigraph to this essay. For now, 'inhabiting a situation' is an adequate formulation for the position of the artist after the 'death of the author' and the birth of the reader, as well as after the simultaneous demise of the modernist subject in favour of something like Beckett's 'unnamable last person I', a favourite of Douglas. It also describes the position of the engaged viewer who endorses the incompleteness of subjectivity as individual only. Betty/Helen, then, is such an unnamable last person I. This is one meaning of the opening scene of the play, where she is being assaulted with electroshocks, as part of her psychiatric 'cure'.[20] Douglas's agency as an artist *inhabits the situation,* the history of his time; or rather, his time including its rewritten, 'preposterous' history. To flesh out this inhabitation, images are frequently combined with spoken words. As in *Der Sandmann*, where the speaking voices are reading a sequence of letters, *Overture's* collage of phantom ride shots of entering and exiting railway tunnels is accompanied by a voice reading a literary montage. This text is composed of passages from Marcel Proust's child-self entering and exiting sleep at the beginning of *A la recherche du temps perdu*, and seems particularly apt for the kind of historiography Douglas performs in this work.

> When I awoke in the middle of the night, I could not even be sure at first *who I was*; for it always happened when I awoke like this, and my mind struggled in an unsuccessful attempt to discover *where I was*, everything revolved around me through the darkness: things, places, years. These shifting and confused *gusts of memory* never lasted more than a few seconds; it often happened that in my brief spell of

20. Douglas used the phrase 'inhabiting a situation' in his commentary on Beckett's teleplays. He wrote with utmost precision how the very opposition between 'they' and 'I' is untenable. Beckett's theatrical work, he argues, moves 'from describing to *inhabiting* situations.' See Stan Douglas, 'Goodbye Pork-Pie Hat', in Watson (ed.), op. cit., pp.92–98. Strangely but meaningfully, Beckett's radical doubt about the 'first person' offers a 'preposterous' return to Descartes, saving the philosopher from the clichéd but wrong interpretations of the *cogito*. On *Overture*, see Noam M. Elcott, 'In Search of Lost Space: Stan Douglas' Archaeology of Cinematic Darkness,' pp.151–182 in *October 139*, Winter, 2012. Some of my ideas on *Overture*, phantom rides and the railway in Douglas's work come from my earlier essay, 'Re-: Killing Time', in *Stan Douglas: Past Imperfect Works. 1986–2007*, Hans D. Christ and Iris Dressler (eds) (exh. cat.) Hatje Cantz,

uncertainty as to where I was, I did not distinguish the various suppositions of which it was composed any more than *when we watch a horse running we isolate the successive positions of its body as they appear upon a bioscope.*[21]

This combined cinematic and literary work subtly demonstrates that position of inhabitation, both visually, in the repetitive ride through the tunnels, and acoustically, in the doubly-translated text, from French to English, and from written to spoken. But also, the rides are 'phantoms,' ostensibly not made by any hand, subject to chance; and the text, although taken from a masterpiece of world literature, is nothing but a cut-and-pasted fragment, written by someone else, appropriated for inhabitation but not for the making of a new 'first person'. In spite of the use of the pronoun 'I,' this 'unnamable last person' emerges from the movement: in and out. Both in and out; on the motion of 'gusts of memory'. This is a form of subjectivity that fits our time better than Proust's modernist own. The subject, here, exists only by virtue of yielding to the waves of time. The passage from Proust, predicting a postmodern sensibility, gives density to the idea of heterochrony.[22]

Phantom rides are, however, not quite subject to chance, but rather to the risks and hazards of the railway – including the capitalist system, the near-slavery its building allowed, and the workers from different other continents it needed and exploited. In North America as elsewhere, the railway has functioned as a tool for the systematization of social-political relations. It was a tool for the establishment of a fierce social hierarchy based on capital, and of the culture of travel that, today, has all but merged with the culture of migration. In North America, the railway also facilitated the conquest of 'the West' by exploiting people from the East. A photograph of an Asian man posing in front of a cardboard cut-out of a cowboy, titled *Passe-tête, 1946*, poignantly shows this triple historicity: the persistence of the past of the beginning of cinema and rail travel, of the post-war years, and of today. Because 'today' not only *has* a past, it always

Stuttgart, 2007, pp.64–93. I return to them now in order to develop them further, and with specific reference to *Helen Lawrence*.

**21.** The text has been pieced together from Marcel Proust, *Remembrance of Things Past*, vol. 1, trans. C.K. Scott Moncrieff and Terence Kilmartin, Penguin Books, London, 1981, pp.6–7; the emphasis is mine. Douglas also uses literature in voice-over in *Der Sandmann*, with only one reader, Nathanael, visible on screen.

**22.** For a contextual and methodological analysis of phantom rides, see Verhoeff, op. cit., pp.282–95, and her *Mobile Screens: The Visual Regime of Navigation*, Amsterdam University Press, Amsterdam, 2012, pp.51–72. In *Overture*, this doubling received yet another layer, as the snowy quality of the old footage over-determines the snow in the landscapes.

Sergeant Leonard Perkins and Henry/Hank Williams

already *is* one. This photograph evokes a moment when labour migration created forms of cultural blending riddled with inequities that today's so-called multicultural societies are still grappling with – with less and less success, it seems.[23]

The 'conquest' has left its imprint both on media culture and on political culture, a combination of central importance for Douglas's work. The 'Chinaman' as he would be called in the early 1900s, was the ancestor of the 1946 Asian cowboy semi-cheerfully yet somewhat uneasily looking at the future – seeing the Vietnam war already looming, perhaps – and today's subsequently mixed world. This is how the early 1900s and the early 2000s overlap through the mediation of that post-war moment in which Douglas places his fiction: the cinema and the railway deployed as machines of conquest converge with the use of media today. The crude painting on the board shows the cowboy as a killer, his fresh victim on the floor, the smoking gun still in his hand. In this way, the Asian man is willy-nilly made complicit with the killing that was the price for the conquest of the West, of the colonization of such large parts of the world, and of the building of the railway. Again, then, media history – here, the way photography superseded painting – cannot be disentangled from social history. *Passe-tête* and *Overture* can thus both be considered programmatic for Douglas's visual philosophy of history, of which *Helen Lawrence* demonstrates the sophisticated culmination.[24]

Erika Balsom cleverly opens her book on exhibiting film, devoted to the recent move of film to the gallery, with *Overture* as her example. In an engaging analysis of the discourse of medium specificity that I have no space to develop here, but which can be fruitfully brought to bear on Douglas's work as a whole and on *Overture* in particular, she remarks on the use, in contemporary artistic practices she calls 'the othered cinema,' of 16mm film 'as a medium aligned with historicity.' This is the function of the projections, in black and white, on the scrim in *Helen Lawrence*, thickened by the visible fact that the images of the characters and actions are shot by digital video cameras *right now*. Balsom also notices that the choice of the Proustian text invokes the *movements* of

23. The dark building with its many dark windows in Douglas's photograph *Ballantyne Pier, 8 June 1935* (2008) is in fact an old sugar refinery, still in operation. The dead appearance of the dark windows might hide a crowd, indeed.

24. Verhoeff offers a detailed account of these intersections between political ('pioneering') and media history (Verhoeff, 2006, op.cit.) In the middle of the twentieth century, Asians could also be part of the Japanese population. See Douglas's work *Pursuit, Fear, Catastrophe: Ruskin BC* (1993) for an evocation. Japanese were frequently confined in the American version of concentration camps. Even a somewhat official publication such as that published by the Japanese American National Museum

involuntary memory – something that is both radically subject-bound and yet, open to chance, hence, at risk. This combination has a strong presence in Douglas's work. This is the real topic of *Helen Lawrence's* seemingly simple *noir* plot. The movement of dense time, here, occurs between the live images on stage that show bodies in actual movement, and the multiplied movements on the projection screen coming from different cameras, miraculously edited on the spot. These images must be seen simultaneously.[25]

This simultaneity is not a boasting of what is technically possible, even if it is awesome what you actually see. But this feeling of awe serves the purpose of conveying a philosophy of time and history as rigorously non-linear. As David Campany rightly remarks: 'In a world economy with its uneven flow of goods, labor, art and information, an understanding of simultaneity becomes a matter of great urgency.' The understanding of simultaneity is, however, complicated by the historical layering. This dense temporality is the key to a revision of what has become an impoverished view of globalisation. The play, and seen with it as a vantage point, the early work, then, does not allow any escape from the multimedia nature of historical time and its political consequences. Here we reach a key point of Douglas's work, hinted at in the early *Overture,* but never so complexly and yet clearly demonstrated as in *Helen Lawrence.*[26]

The political importance of understanding history in simultaneity that Campany recommends can be seen in a more specific way, equally pointing to the bond between media and politics through history and narrative. This specification is three-tiered.

First, as is well known, in many countries foreign films are not subtitled but dubbed. This means that, even in the best of cases, the body of the actor is separated from the voice. This is unfortunate, including politically, because disembodying diminishes the communicative impact of speech. We are no longer the second person to whom the actor speaks, even indirectly in the case of fictional dialogue. The voice is disembodied and becomes something else, sometimes like a commentary or even an accidental scrap of discourse floating by.

acknowledges the analogy of the 'internment camps' to concentration camps. See Brian Niiya, *Japanese American History: An A-to-Z Reference from 1868 to the Present*, Facts On File, New York, 1993. The heydays were the 1950s – the working years of Douglas's fictional photographer.

25. Erika Balsom, *Exhibiting Cinema in Contemporary Art*, Amsterdam University Press, Amsterdam, 2013, p.2. For a very illuminating view of medium specificity brought to bear on the distinction between film and video, not as (essentialised) media but as practices, see Janna Houwen, *Mapping Moving Media: Film and Video*, PhD dissertation, University of Leiden, 2014.

26. Campany, in Krempel, op. cit., p.14.

Buddy Black and Betty Mansfield/Helen Lawrence

Also, secondly, dubbing supposedly saves spectators the effort, but also deprives them of the opportunity, of reading and seeing simultaneously. Too bad, though, because watching a film with subtitles means practising the art of simultaneous understanding. More keenly political, this now generalised practice, also on television, is an effective tool for censorship. Language can be softened, harsh discourse mitigated, even distorted. More specifically still, thirdly, dubbing can be used quite concretely as a weapon. In an essay on Irish performance art, Christa-Maria Lerm Hayes recalls that 'IRA members were interviewed and voiced-over by actors, who were eventually to speak their lines a-synchronously to the lip movements, so as to break empathy and de-humanize.' Simultaneity, or synch, then, becomes a form of resistance in itself. And so can, within it, the presence of the body in speech.[27]

In view of Douglas's elaboration of the dense time of history, the fact that in *Helen Lawrence* the simultaneity is almost miraculous, and chronologically reversed in the sense that we see the projections with their historical aesthetic first, and only with effort, 'behind' it, the acting in the present, makes this point even more forcefully – its politics less anecdotal and more general. But what is really the radical sting of *Helen Lawrence,* in terms of simultaneity as the mode of engaging history in and for the present, is the unheard-of visual simultaneity. Doubly implicating time – in the historicising projections over-layering the contemporary actors, and in the movement that is a feature of both theatre and film – the two tracks of the play 'stay in synch,' in order to foreground the simultaneity itself. But 'synch,' here, is not a technological issue of matching video and audio tracks; everything stays in synch because it is live: the actors on stage are being composited into the virtual sets in real time. 'Real time' seems miraculous, simply because it is indeed real. This is a very meaningful gesture, of metaphor made real. Simultaneity, in the convergence of media already staged in *Overture*, is a medium in itself. It is one that enables history to stay with us, so that a future may be possible.

Nanna Verhoeff, whose project is precisely the analysis of such convergence of old and new media, writes in her recent book on contemporary mobility and its historical roots, making sense of Douglas's deployment of travel as spacetime:

> The cinematic phantom ride and the mobile screen have in common that they not only display but also constitute an

27. Christa-Maria Lerm Hayes, 'Sandra Johnston: Doubt, Gesture, Love and the Paradoxes of (Political) Art in Northern Ireland', in Sandra Johnston, *Beyond Reasonable Doubt: An Investigation of Doubt, Risk and Testimony Through Performance Art Processes in Relation to Systems of Legal Justice,* European Studies in Culture and Policy, Dublin, 2014, p.13.

experience of travel. … Both deploy the imagery of travel to underscore the (new) medium's capacity as a virtual travel machine. The dynamic of travel as topic-trope-metaphor results in a mirror image or synecdoche – specifically in the form of a *mise-en-abyme* – when the medium in the image comes to stand for the mobility of the image. This shift from a thematic to a metaphoric reflection of mobility is visible throughout the history of media. I am referring in particular to those moments when physical mobility was first used to establish and demonstrate the virtual mobility of the medium.[28]

And Verhoeff goes on to analyse several types of such films characterized by a 'first-person point of view shot' in ways that would foreground the kind of historicity of Douglas's deployment of the genre in *Overture*. *Overture* is invoked here as an allegorical statement of Douglas's sense of history as heterochronous and multiply-layered, in this respect prefiguring *Helen Lawrence* while the literary element, also strongly present in *Der Sandmann,* adds to this intricate multiplicity. Prefiguring post-structuralist visions of subjectivity, Proust, in the fragments Douglas chooses so well for *Overture*, opens subjectivity up to outside forces that no one can master – hence, the importance of chance, characteristic of a certain modernism that counters the individualism easily implied by the foregrounding of subjectivity, as Robert Caserio has analyzed for literature and Mary Ann Doane for cinema.[29]

It is in this crux that modernism (Proust) and postmodernism (Douglas) join forces. The fragments of Proust foreground the movement – a whirlwind like in his image of the dancer; he felicitously calls it '*gusts* of memory' – of 'things, places, years.' And as in early photography, he writes, 'when we watch a horse running, we isolate the successive positions of its body as they appear upon a bioscope.' Proust is probably unaware of this allusion to Marey, Muybridge who was commissioned to test Marey's results, and Degas who was either influenced by Muybridge or not.

The reference to 'gusts of wind' in the description of the peculiar involuntary memory, which Proust's passage suggests is an index of sleep, opens an entire cluster of philosophical thoughts that are closely connected to Douglas's audio-visual theorizing of heterotemporality. In an in-depth discussion of Charles S. Peirce's concept of the index, Doane formulates the *event*

28. Verhoeff, 2012, op. cit., p.60.

29. See Robert Caserio, *The Novel in England 1900–1950: History and Theory*, Twayne Publishers, New York, 1999 and Mary Ann Doane, *The Emergence of Cinematic Time: Modernity, Contingency, the Archive*, Harvard University Press, Cambridge, MA, 2002.

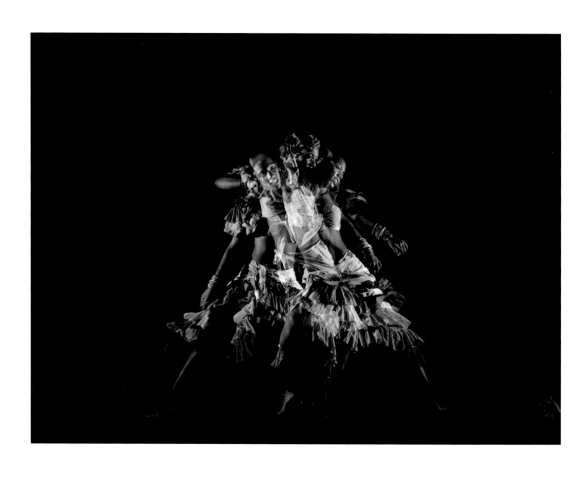

*Midcentury Studio: Dancer II, 1950*, 2010
Digital fibre print mounted on Dibond aluminium
152.4 x 184.8 x 7 cm

of indexicality in terms that fit the threshold between sleep and non-sleep Proust evokes:

> They [indices] are dependent upon certain unique contingencies: the *wind blowing* at the moment in a certain direction, a foot having landed in the mud at precisely this place, the camera shutter opening at a given time. Unlike icons, indices have no resemblance to their objects, which, nevertheless, directly cause them. ... [The index] *is a hollowed-out sign.*[30]

In addition to her insistence on singularity – Doane phrases this as 'unique contingencies' – her examples of such indexical events bring together place, camera, and the unique moment, or instant, in that fugitive element, the wind. The instant is that of the present – a contentious issue in the philosophy of time at the beginning of the twentieth century. In view of this discussion, the moment when, in *Helen Lawrence*, the stage remains the blue room but the projection shows two men outside with strongly presented white clouds behind them, moving from left to right, can very well be read as such an indexical presence of 'gusts of wind' as indicating the motor of time. But this is slow time, in the sense of duration; the clouds don't storm by but move ever so slowly, a movement only visible for those eager, willing and able to see duration as moving.[31]

In quite a few photographs from Douglas's *Midcentury Studio*, it is less legs we see running, as in Proust's fragment, but hands that we see trying to give chance a hand, so to speak. In *Clown, 1946* (p.77), we have seen the importance of the thumb. In *Dancer II, 1950*, the hand is also crucial. The hand is the tool of tricks, as in *Clown*, and the tool of crime – theft, in *Cache, 1948* (p.31), gambling, in *Dice, 1950* (p.27) – respectively. In both cases, the combination of chance, significant in modernist fiction, and precariousness, central in post-war societies, forges the idea of risk.

These two motives come together in *Cache, 1948*, where the risk taken by petty crime is supposedly mastered by the subsequent wealth, indicated here as illusory: the cigar

---

30. Doane, op. cit., p.92 (the emphasis is mine).

31. Neither Peirce nor Bergson believed in the instant, however, because, as Deleuze wrote, 'Bergsonian duration is defined less by succession than by coexistence.' See Gilles Deleuze, *Bergsonism*, trans. Hugh Tomlinson and Barbara Habberjam, Zone Books, New York, 1988, p.60. Coexistence is characteristic both for video installation where multiple screens coexist, and for heterochrony, where multiple 'slices of time' coexist. Bergson's philosophy of the image is already heterochronic. See Henri Bergson, *Matter and Memory*, trans. N. M. Paul and W. S. Palmer, Zone Books, New York, 1991, 1896.

suggests the high-society life that the content of the cache and petit-bourgeois interior (indicated by the radiator and the flowered wallpaper) appear to contradict. But the cigar is extinct, and due to frequent use (indexing crime as everyday routine), the flowered wallpaper is frayed and dirty around the edges of the hidden space and its cover. Inside are all the forbidden, illegal items: money, booze, dominos, cigars, and dice. The hand steals, the hand hides, and the hand reveals. With its cigar, the hand dreams. And the link becomes explicit in the tense hand throwing dice in *Dice, 1950*, isolating the man in the middle from the three identically-hatted men as the one who, in this moment, is at risk, while the dice are frozen, like the clown's orange, in mid-air, albeit blurred in this case.

Douglas complicates history in many different ways. *Midcentury Studio*, the photographs that are fictionally the product of a photographer who, in that ominous year 1945, could easily have been an army veteran, and whose existence in the following years would remain precarious as well as culturally creative, is one of his experiments with the exploration of heterochrony. A first feature of a heterochronic conception of history is a temporal layeredness or density, to which Douglas owns up by means of his double act of dating the works. Moreover, the photographs are amazingly precise in their styling according to mid-twentieth century conventions, yet also clearly of today in their large format and digital printing. Thus they forge a bond of solidarity between the two moments. This is what makes us ponder: which utopian visions of that earlier moment turned out lost, or falsified; what other futures would have been possible? Through suggesting such pondering, the artist revises, complicates, and undermines linear time. He also posits history as the royal, or at least, the only possible road to the future.

This is how Douglas is a historian, able to suggest convergences between so many domains of society, including especially the media that both function in it as well as mirror it. This integration makes the important point that art is not positioned outside of society but at the heart of it, participating in it. This includes subjectivity, precarious and unnamable as it is, instead of being opposed to it. This is why the expressions of subjectivity as transient, divided, and always in the process of negotiation (the shadow) in *Malabar People* are so crucial for an understanding of Douglas's conception of history. It is also one of the functions of the evocations of war and its aftermath in *Helen Lawrence*. This motif saves the plot from the banality of its precedents in *film noir*.

For example, early on Walker/Wallace (the man hiding from and searched for by Betty/Helen) criticizes the corrupt police chief Muldoon. But he is not blaming him for bothering Eva with what we now call sexual harassment. Instead, he says:

'You shouldn't have been going on about her old man. He's got shell shock'. But Muldoon, the narcissistic bully, only has this to answer: 'Hell, who doesn't? You got shot up, you got over it. Don't hear you whining about it.' Walker continues: 'Yeah, you never know when it's gonna back up and bite you. Give the kid a break.' What Walker, who seems otherwise totally cynical and as much a profiteer as Muldoon, is insisting on is the ongoing risk involved in war veterans living among 'us'. The war's over, is said here and there. But it isn't; for time, in the wake of trauma, cannot move on. In the middle of a stereotypical fiction, then, historical reality comes, indeed, back to bite us. Thus, Douglas the historian of heterochrony merges with Douglas the visual philosopher of time, subjectivity, and visual art in their social impact.


## Narrator – Narratologist

This complex intertwined history is possible thanks to the one central feature of history that every historian uses but often fails to reflect on: narrativity. I have always worked on and with narrative, including Proust. Theorizing narrative was my primary specialization, and from this admittedly partial perspective I find Douglas's works totally fascinating. His work is narrative in radically new ways, which impact on the kind of history his work images. For this, we are best off starting at what appears to be the other side of narrative, namely abstraction.[32]

Consider what is narrative about, say, *Intrigue, 1948*. This image is as close to abstraction as narrativity can come. Qua iconography, this chaos-structure, to invoke yet another paradox, an impenetrable Moebius strip, is identical to the one that occupies the right-bottom corner of a four-part section of cases in Henri Cartier-Bresson's *Natcho Aguirre, Santa Clara, Mexico* (p.114) from 1934, only accessible in a print from 1946. Cartier-Bresson's work is a worthy reference, or allusion: at the time he was under the spell of surrealism and made many brilliant works of veiled faces and bodies. And like Douglas, but in real time, a dozen years later he was deeply

32. On narrative, see Mieke Bal, *Narratology: Introduction to the Theory of Narrative* (3rd edition), University of Toronto Press, Toronto, 2009. On Proust, with an emphasis on his visualizing writing, see Mieke Bal, *The Mottled Screen: Reading Proust Visually*, trans. Anna-Louise Milne, Stanford University Press, Stanford, CA, 1997. Abstraction has been looming over Douglas's work, and the current series of *Corrupt Files* (2013) (pp.2–3, 5, 7, 151, 153–55). In *A Thousand Plateaus*, Deleuze theorises the notion of abstraction to mean the opening up of new possible forms, rather than a refusal of form. See Gilles Deleuze and Félix Guattari, *A Thousand Plateaus: Capitalism and Schizophrenia*, trans. Brian Massumi, Athlone Press, London, 1987.

Mary Jackson and Rose George

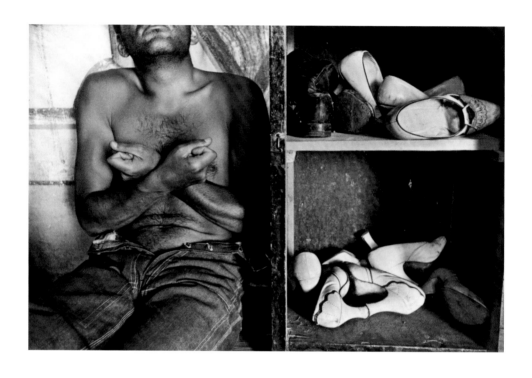

Henri Cartier-Bresson, *Natcho Aguirre, Santa Clara, Mexico*, 1934

engaged with the post-war period. They both explored the fine line between surreal obfuscation and magic – *Midcentury Studio* has many photographs of magical tricks, and seen from this angle, others, such as the *Dancer II, 1950* (p.108) and even *Cache, 1948* (p.31) can be seen in this light. And the most incredible tour de force of magic is *Helen Lawrence* as a whole.

Abstraction can be seen as another form of magic, a form from where new possibilities arise. Douglas abstracts the pair of shoes from the more directly narrative clutter in Cartier-Bresson's image in his photograph *Intrigue, 1948* (p.29). A pair of high-heeled shoes, set on a reflecting surface, and pointing their noses in opposite directions: this evokes, but does not represent a dance floor. The composition is wilfully over-the-top precise: whose dancing feet would twist so precisely, and their reflection so clearly *still*? Moreover, the disposition of the shoes is such that left and right are reversed. No feet, even of the most brilliant dancer, can do this. Besides, there are no feet inside the shoes.[33]

Although everything suggests that a pair of shoes is reflected in a mirroring surface, the blackness of that surface makes it impossible to discern a mirror. On the shoes' surfaces, just more sheen, potentially reflecting in their turn. What is the intrigue of the title, then, that term that invokes the plotting and planning of the shady characters in *Helen Lawrence,* but also, more in general, evokes narrative plot? I think of Deleuze's concept of abstraction as the possibility of figuration. Similarly, but with a twist, this work seamlessly merges the narrative notion of intrigue with the everyday idea of curiosity attached to the qualifier 'intriguing'. The combined meaning of this still image, then, is the *possibility of narrative.* This is Douglas's own brand of abstraction, dialoguing with Deleuze's philosophical view. It establishes a bond between his movie and video works and the still photographs. And guess what? 'Intrigue' is just the name of the shoes' brand.[34]

Things happen, in time and place, and any account of them – in words, images, films, or combinations thereof – is narrative. This is challenging, especially when using still images to 'tell' stories. Yet, if we want to know how time produces narrativity in still images, one look at *Clown, 1946* suffices. Capturing its movement in a still image foregrounds the chrono-logic of photography; it states that photography is *by definition*, not only in the special efforts to capture time, chrono-photography. Thus, by way of this work, Douglas theorizes still images as narrative and, hence, moving. This, as I have argued elsewhere through reference to Bergson, pertains to a philosophy of the image, memory, and the fundamentally heterochronic nature of time.[35]

The heterochronic nature of time has a decisive impact on the image, and *Clown* visually explains why. In *Matter and Memory* Bergson suggests that living in duration is a form of gathering: each moment is accompanied by the memory of preceding ones, not necessarily in the chronological or causal order of their occurrence. Perception involves both the materiality of objects and of

33. The photograph *Shoes, 1947,* preceding *Intrigue, 1948,* in the catalogue of *Midcentury Studio* (Simoens, op. cit.), shows the impossibility of dance in an opposite way. Here, there are feet, but they don't fit the shoes. For the Cartier-Bresson image and many other relevant ones, see the recent catalogue, Clément Chéroux, *Henri Cartier-Bresson: Here and Now,* Thames and Hudson, London, 2014, p.105, cat. no. 83.

34. See Deleuze and Guattari, op. cit. I have developed this notion of abstraction in chapter 5 of my *Endless Andness: The Politics of Abstraction According to Ann Veronica Janssens,* op. cit. .

35. See the introduction to my *Thinking in Film: The Politics of Video Art Installation According to Eija-Liisa Ahtila,* op. cit.

Chief James Muldoon and Sergeant Leonard Perkins

the human body. Bergson considers the body to be a material entity, and he consequently sees perception as a material practice. Perception is not a construction but a selection, of and for the body. Selection is also the principle of framing. Photography, then, is a selection offered for further selection, on the basis of solidarity between artistic agency and viewer. Given Bergson's insistence on the inseparability of time and space, the image is also by definition in movement. It is material, not because of the support we associate with images, but because the bodily action of mobilizing the image is material. Hence, 'still' images also move.[36]

There is no context to read any of these images fully; hence, the viewer is left to her own devices; to her own understanding of and feeling for heterochrony. At the other end of the line the index traces in *Smoke, 1947*, for example, we see something white – a cigarette butt, perhaps? But the suggestion – confirmed by the ornate contraption in which the white detail lies – that this is a festive occasion spoiled but not killed by a master of ceremony is countered by the amount of smoke no cigarette butt will easily produce. Something happens, and the authoritarian or moralizing hand may be a fearful warning; the story gains in suspense. Never mind what the 'truth' of the image is. The sheer fact that we can, however briefly, hesitate about the meaning of the pointing finger is enough to realize how this image activates the act of viewing. In this way, suspense is turned by 90 degrees, from the flat image to the interaction between image and viewer.

The heart of classical narrative is suspense. Douglas is a master in the creation of narrative suspense, as well as of the productive frustration caused by the lack of resolution. The lack of resolution of the plot of *Helen Lawrence* is, in this respect, the clearest indication that the staging of period style and the espousing of period genre such as *film noir* are not simple returns to history but tools to work with in order to unsettle easily satisfying narratives. I'd even consider those styles and the technology required to make it, media. Suspense, yes; resolution, no. Here lies another function of the invocation of war traumatism. About two-thirds into the play, the following dialogue occurs. Eva has been to see a doctor – we were led to believe she was getting an illegal abortion. But to her husband, war veteran Edward, she says it was on his behalf. Given that the decision to not keep the child is inspired by her despair over her marriage with the traumatised Edward, the two are inseparable.

36. See Henri Bergson, op.cit..

37. There is no space to go into this important issue. See my film made with Michelle Williams Gamaker, *A Long History of Madness* (2011). For background, see my article 'Spatialising

Eva: I was saying they [young doctors with a new approach] listen to you.
They let you talk and tell them about what you saw in the war.
Edward: But things can't be unseen. Things can't be undone.
Eva: He can help you put it out of your mind.
Edward: As if there never was a war.
Eva: As if there is a future.
Edward: Is there? ...
Eva: You were full of hope.
Edward: I guess I sprung a leak.

The kind of witty repartee in the last bit binds this dialogue to the *film noir* tradition. And the play is full of such clever jokes. To use this ploy here insures that the discussion of trauma is not disconnected from the rest of the play, doesn't become clinical, and doesn't participate in the trauma industry in cultural studies. Stylistically and aesthetically it remains anchored in the specificity of its time.

The bit before that joke must be considered with a view of verb tense. 'As if there never was' versus 'as if there is': the past perfect, or in Douglas's terms (see p.122ff), past imperfect of unreal, nostalgically invoked impossibility – things cannot be undone, nor unseen – is subtly opposed to the real possibility of a future, conditioned as it is upon our way of dealing with the past – think of another function for abstraction. In a nutshell, we have here the entire discussion in Freudian psychoanalysis about the question of whether psychosis (of which traumatised states are a case) can be healed through analysis. Freud didn't think so. Contemporary analysts fruitfully experiment with methods to contradict him. Here, Edward and Eva don't succeed in dealing with the former's war trauma. I speculate it is because the futurality expressed in the play with tenses does not acknowledge the stagnation of time that is trauma. As a result, Edward will soon be brandishing his service gun, after trying in vain to sell it. Suspense: will he begin a killing spree, or kill himself, as traumatised war veterans are wont to do? No answer.[37]

This abduction of suspense for a staging of trauma is the simplest but also the most adequate way of describing the nature of Douglas's narratives. It is also a way of engaging the history of narrative critically. Of the images of *Midcentury Studio, Suspect, 1950* (p.25) is the most suspenseful. Three men sit in the back of a car. Two men with hats on flank the middle

Film', in *Hunting High and Low. Festschrift for Jostein Gripsrud*, Jan Fredrik Hovden and Karl Knapskog (eds), Scandinavian Academic Press, Oslo, pp.160–82, 2012. Douglas's engagement with psychoanalysis in *Der Sandmann* suggests that this association is not unwarranted.

Edward and Eva Banks

one with sunglasses. This man is the only one looking in the direction of the viewer, but due to the sunglasses we don't see his eyes. It is perhaps the most 'scary' image of the series. The man in the middle is already captured, and likely to end up in a lake with his feet in concrete, 'getting the boot'; or, if he is lucky and the title is meaningful, in prison. Getting the boot can mean this mafiosi murdering method, but also being fired, losing your job, as is the threat hovering over the characters in *Helen Lawrence* from the beginning and, since there is no resolution, beyond the end.

When I think about Douglas's creation of suspense, I'd like again to return to an early work, one of his mono-dramas from the early 1990s. One of these is suspenseful – the one titled *I'm not Gary*. Here, a white man addresses a black man in a friendly way, greeting him, as if he knew him: 'Hi Gary'. But he is uncovered as someone who considers all black people identical when the addressee says: 'I'm not Gary'. Both men look rather upset, shocked, or angry. A fight might ensue, or just the humiliation of the white man; either way, this is suspenseful on the basis of our knowledge of a certain racial thinking. Douglas's heterotemporal conception of history is implicated as well. In other words, suspense and social politics are bound up together, as our memory of racism is activated. Thus, in order to resolve the suspense, or even make sense of the short film, we must implicate ourselves.

In this ultra-short monodrama, nothing happens. But the suspense is there. This withholding of contextual information, this suspension of the denouement, the satisfying resolution of the mini-plot or monodrama, is part of Douglas's relation to the cultural, technological, and political past. He knows, and makes us experience, that we always fill in context ourselves, with our knowledge of social situations and previous images – and the fragments Douglas creates for us to stage the past on behalf of the future. This not only points to the ubiquity of visual culture, but also to our own responsibility for what we do in and with that mediated world.

This is how Douglas forges the relation to the past, a relation that the title of the exhibition he had in the Staatsgalerie and the Württembergischer Kunstverein in Stuttgart in 2007–2008, 'Past Imperfect', so brilliantly summed up. Especially in bilingual Canada this pun confusing two verb tenses, '*passé simple*' and '*imparfait*' – the former existing only in French, not in English – will be appreciated. But more profoundly, that title addresses the many ways Douglas establishes a dense relationship with the imperfect past, as situated in the present, in its own imperfection. The idea of an imperfect past as a past imperfect – transforming a remote history into a lived 'tense,' since the 'imparfait' is the tense of a past that endures – makes the point of heterochronic history. The title refers back to the nexus of utopian ideals current at certain moments in the past. The end of World War II was surely a moment rich in such ideals, as was the beginning of the last century. The 'imperfection' makes it possible to imagine an intertwinement of idealist and disabused views. Douglas calls them 'failed utopias'.

In that exhibition in Stuttgart as well as in the current one at The Fruitmarket Gallery, Edinburgh that this publication accompanies, *Vidéo* (2007, pp.125, 126, 129) addresses this issue emphatically. This is a work that ostensibly replies to Samuel Beckett's 1965 film titled *Film*, but in fact responds just as much to Franz Kafka's novel *The Trial* (1925), Orson Welles's eponymous film (1962), and Jean-Luc Godard's *Deux ou trois choses que je sais d'elle* (Two or Three Things I Know about Her, 1966). Like Beckett's *Film*, but unlike *The Trial*, Douglas's *Vidéo* only shows the main character from the back. The film is also very dark; in this it is one of Douglas's works that reshapes the gothic for today, passing through the 1950s then-update of the gothic in *film noir*. As a response to Beckett's film, a triple identity swap has taken place. The white older man is now a black young woman. Like Beckett's O (from 'object'), she tears up family photographs, which she carries in a similar folder to the one O has. Presumably, as far as the narrative impulse dictates our viewing, since she is sitting in the space of the archive, these are pictures of her in her birth family. That guess emerges out of our narrative habits; it's how narrativity works.[38]

Although the scene is practically identical to a scene towards the end in Beckett's *Film*, where the man contemplates, caresses, and then tears up a happy-family photograph, the change to a young woman, which brings the video closer to Godard's film, transforms the imagined *narrative* played out. In addition to reflecting on medium history, this scene of *Vidéo*, one imagines, might refer to an adoption story. This plot of adoption and the search for roots as the basis of identity is very much of our time. So is another allusion to possible plots, this one not derived from *Film*: during the first nightly visit of the detective, the woman offers him her passport, as if she needs to justify that her presence is 'legal'. Such scenes set *Vidéo* in the realm of the contemporary, with its violent immigration policy that declares people

38. Substituting a black young woman for an ageing white man is a typical gesture. Douglas changed gender before (e.g. in his *Journey into Fear*, 2001). The three changes in the character in *Vidéo* – two compared to *The Trial* – make sense in terms of the precise contemporariness of the work. Moreover, the symmetry is enhanced by the reference of Godard's film, the third intertext, where the main character is a young white woman. This almost completes the list of possible identities in terms of race, age, and gender. The only ones missing are the older and the younger black man. Part of these paragraphs on *Vidéo* come from my earlier essay, 'Re-: Killing Time', in Christ and Dressler, op. cit., pp.64–93. I recycle these bits of that essay because they are key to my argument here.

'illegal' – a contemporariness that is re-actualized by the persecution topic of *The Trial*. These are two of many ways in which the work intervenes in historical time.

In responding to these two different cinematic texts, Douglas's work offers a new, narratively-inflected answer to the question of how a political art is possible that does not depend on the many traps that caused the demise of the critique of ideology, and how playing with narrativity – a time machine – can help create such art. As Douglas does so often, a third moment is brought in to intensify the heterochronicity. The moment of the 1960s, the time of the artist's childhood and the time when the three films engaged in *Vidéo* were made, is perhaps the hidden, or secret, historical moment of failed utopias Douglas's work addresses. This was the moment when, in the wake of Adorno – who is more precisely a contemporary of Douglas's fictional photographer of the 1940s – we believed in the critique of ideology as a remedy to the social-cultural ills towards which we developed a certain paranoia.

Of the failed visions of that time, which have not disappeared today, the most obvious are the following, and Douglas counters them all, acknowledging their enduring presence: the 'othering' illusion that one can avoid ideology – that only others hold ideologies, which 'we' can then critique; the didactic belief in consciousness-raising; the confusion of or unreflected transfer between social and psychoanalytical issues; the contempt for aesthetics based on an unwarranted ideology of artistic autonomy; and the narratological collapse of character and artist. This first one is the reason why in *Helen Lawrence* no character is aloof, or remains innocent of the corruption and its practices. The second one is the reason Douglas's work is never overtly, loudly political, and why there is never a clear answer to the dilemmas staged. While compelling us to think, he doesn't force us to think what he thinks. The third one is the reason why psychoanalysis, not foregrounded as such, is frequently present indirectly. Only when it is present can the individualism of subjectivity be countered. *Der Sandmann* is the clearest allusion to that body of theory, and in *Helen Lawrence,* the issue of war traumatism hints at it. But the avoidance of an individualising approach to psychoanalysis makes the works always more complex and dense, never mono-disciplinary. The fourth failed vision, the contempt for the aesthetic, is barred by the extreme formal perfection of the works, always in the service of a social issue that deserves this aesthetic homage. The last one is the reason I began by setting the person Stan Douglas aside.

In Douglas's *Vidéo* the necessary in-betweenness that his intertextual relationship to three political films of the 1960s drives home, is elaborated on all possible levels: from aesthetic 'look' to philosophical tenor, from technological to exhibitionary modes, from suspense narrative and the suspension of its ending, and

still from **Vidéo**, 2007
High definition single channel video installation
colour, sound, 18:11 mins (loop)

still from **Vidéo**, 2007

from one spectatorial position to another. It is in a multiple return movement, a repetition that the artist moves forward, to articulate a political form of art beyond modernism and its utopias. His tool for this is that certain kind of narrativity without denouement I mentioned above. This alternative is anchored in re-mediated history and re-configured narrativity. In short, in acknowledgment of the importance of the past in the present, as I mentioned in the section on the researcher, he deploys the prefix 're-'.

In my essay 'Re-: Killing Time' in the catalogue of the Stuttgart exhibitions mentioned previously. I first developed my argument about Douglas's multiple deployment of 're-' as a primary tool in his projects, one which clearly points to the importance of killing linear time and promoting, instead, heterochronic time. The kind of temporality that ensues is multiple and messy; it invokes a 'pre-posterous' conception of history, in which the past is constantly rewritten in the present and hence is constantly 'on the move'. This makes a transparent reconstruction of the past impossible. Between past art and the present, wrote Svetlana Alpers and Michael Baxandall, later art stands like a screen. They recall the well-known case of Cézanne, whose work we can only see through the screen of Cubism. We can add the allusion to the Lacanian screen – the opacity that fleshes out what we can see through the cultural pre-dispositions that, like language, select and colour our visions for us.[39]

Douglas takes this metaphor of the screen literally in *Helen Lawrence*. The resulting aesthetic is dauntingly successful. But this is not because it is beautiful and consistent – which it also is. More importantly, the subtle differences between the stage and the screen are always meaningful ways of showing how we cannot see without Bergsonian 'gathering'. The moment clouds slowly move between the stage and the projection is not only indexical of the 'gusts of wind' of memory, as I have suggested above, but also of the long tradition of landscape painting. Another moment that sets up media in dialogue is towards the end, when Walker/Wallace is squeezing the life out of Harry, in another murder which replicates the hatpin method that earlier had allowed him to frame Helen for the murder of her husband. Now the stage seems far away, frustratingly, because it is here that the action happens. But on the scrim, we see the close up of Walker/Wallace: impatient, desperate, anxious, with fear in his eyes. With *Vidéo*, the artist retrospectively, or 'preposterously' clarifies his conception of time as he has shaped it in earlier works. With *Helen Lawrence*

**39**. Svetlana Alpers and Michael Baxandall, *Tiepolo and the Pictorial Intelligence*, Yale University Press, London and New Haven, 1994.

he takes these issues up and explores the formal potential they hold, not to devoid the play of meaning but on the contrary, thickening the traditional narrative.

In *Helen Lawrence* the past of the post-war period is given to us twice, simultaneously. And because we see the live performance, albeit sometimes only in silhouettes, the cinematic but also the live images lose their temporal innocence, their illusory *Jetztzeit*, the nowness that makes cinema so seductive because we believe in the presence of what we see whereas it is already the past. When this shimmering history becomes part of the everyday experience, it leads to heterochronic experience. I contend that in the end, this is what Douglas achieves with his special way of creating narrative.[40]

Douglas's narratorial activity is best summed up with his term re-combination. Douglas's re-visiting – or re-cycling – of older images is a project of making the past matter, but not as past alone – not so that the present is a linear consequence of the past, or something that can be disentangled from it. Re-search (or *Recherche*), into the history of cinema, photography, and literature; re-*venant*, the spectres of past politics that haunt the present; and re-sidue, the sticky remainder of the openness of the late 1940s and the illusions of the 1960s, are only the most relevant and visible forms of his re-visiting of history, culture, and technology. His seeing again or re-visioning, targets includes re-pression, of affect by linear narrative, and serves as a re-minder, as the necessary task of art. It constitutes a plea for re-ciprocating, a give-and-take between artworks and between the latter and their respective audiences, a reciprocity whose agency has been paralyzed by the passive-making quality of traditional narrative. These relationships are re-visited to be re-worked through re-petition – of ways of filming, plots, and possibilities of critique. As a result, re-surrection (of the woman shot in *Vidéo*, who comes back to life as the film loops and starts again; of *Midcentury Studio's* veteran-turned-photographer, now long dead; of the old man in *Der Sandmann,* who shifts away into the seam, then returns), and re-lation (between past photos, films and narratives and present ones, and suspensefully, Helen turned Betty). Douglas's alternative to re-presentation is re-configuration and re-combination. These are effective tools to make art that works. Research, history and narrative – my three interests in Douglas's work so far – come together in *Vidéo*, in *Der Sandmann*, in the photographs of *Midcentury Studio*, and in *Helen Lawrence*, all in different ways.

As part of the endeavour to reset the work in the contemporary realm but carrying

---

40. *Jetztzeit* is best explained in the fifth thesis of Walter Benjamin, 'Thesis on the Philosophy of History', in Arendt, *Illuminations*, op. cit., pp.253–64

still from *Vidéo*, 2007

along its pastness, *Vidéo* is not only shot in digital video but also in colour. We see very little of the colours, however, since all the scenes are extremely dark, in a literalisation of the *film noir* aesthetic. The superimposition of black-and-white projection over colour in the live performance in *Helen Lawrence* unpacks this aesthetic of *Vidéo,* making its double layering explicit. As a result of both that darkness and the large projection, the digitally-produced image looks grainy.[41]

This makes the video literally both black-and-white and colour, merging past and present moving images; prefiguring the radical double-layeredness of the media in *Helen Lawrence*. As for colour, there are patches of red and blue, in the woman's surroundings, and there is green for her. It is the colour of her character's jacket and sweater. When all else recedes to black, we still see that green jacket. The use of video and of colour, while displaying the work like a film in a single-screen installation and almost making the colour disappear, is a deliberate updating-within-history of Beckett's *Film* as well as Welles's *Trial*; deliberate, especially for an artist with so many black-and-white films to his name. This treatment of both medium and display mode is programmatic; it tells us something important about video, specifically, in installation, and how it re-combines narrativity with social issues. This installation aspect adds to the activation of viewers to make their own plot.

There is a multiply forking narrativity, here, as well, and again thanks to hands – and to a typical Douglassian 're-' – namely the form of the video loop. The first time I saw *Vidéo*, on entering the dark space I thought I saw a hand go down, then heard a gunshot, then disco music. When I subsequently saw, from a high and distant point of view, the young woman walk on a plaza in a bleak suburb of Paris, on a rainy night, I thought she had fired the shot. Soon afterwards she receives a nightly visit from two detectives, and begins her descent into hell. Luckily, I had entered at the end. This film is really looped (based on re-), however, without credits interrupting it. So, it welcomes viewers entering at any moment. This is one of the ways the video defies linear time. Once the analogy with *The Trial* became clear I had to surrender to the possibility that she got shot – but I could never visually ascertain this.

**41.** Information from the Douglas studio about the production of *Vidéo* revealed that the grainy quality was due to the fact that the gain on the HD video camera was set to +12 dB for the entire shoot. This gives the camera three extra stops of exposure, but it also introduces the noise from the CCD – it is always there, even when there is no light, as if the imaging panel were seeing itself seeing. The three colours

If I have spent some time on *Vidéo* in this reflection on narrativity, it is not because, as a suspenseful work of moving images, this work would 'naturally' be more strongly narrative than the still photographs in the current exhibition. Instead, I aim to prepare the ground for an assessment of the specific kind of narrativity in still images. This narrativity binds research and history to art's political force. But please remember the paradoxical narrativity of *Intrigue, 1948* (p.29), that owed its effectivity to its proximity to abstraction. I will now turn to another paradox, to claim that the political force of Douglas's work resides primarily in its deployment of fictionality.

## Fiction-Maker

In spite of, or rather, because of his strong commitment to history, Douglas is also a maker or re-combiner of fictions. Fictionality must be interwoven into the other topics discussed so far in order for them to really work. Having wrestled with views of fiction that characterize it as separated from reality – in parallel worlds, as in Possible World Theory, for example – I have been attracted by the rather old view (first proposed by Coleridge) of fictionality as 'the willing suspension of disbelief.' What remains powerful in that view is the 'willingness,' which implies that the viewer plays along, knows what she does, and hence, is not manipulated; that suspension, not cancellation is the attitude, so that the viewer is not permanently dulled into a facile passivity; and the focus is on 'disbelief,' not belief.

What is suspended, not cancelled – willingly, not compellingly – is the reality-testing attitude of permanent suspicion and search for the truth. Instead, fiction opens up to new possibilities. In that sense it is comparable to abstraction. Fiction is to reality what abstraction is to figuration. Indispensible, it makes newness possible in a world stagnating with clichés. In my own activities this power of fiction has drawn me to a long-term project of a fiction film on a very real social issue, mental illness or 'madness'. Fictionality, in this project, serves a purpose congenial to Freud's 'theoretical fiction', *Totem and Taboo* (1913). Speculating on what might plausibly have happened,

– green, blue and red – are the primary colours video uses to make all colours. For an artwork that makes this theory of colour its basis, see Ann Veronica Janssens's installation *Blue, Red and Yellow* (2001) and later versions of this work. See Balsom's 2013 study for the many consequences of this contemporary mode of installation of the re-use of cinema (Balsom, op. cit.).

Harry Mitchell and Percy Walker/Wallace

*Midcentury Studio: Burlap, 1948*, 2010
Digital fibre print mounted on Dibond aluminium
73.7 x 90.5 x 4.4 cm

Freud's fictional search for origins enabled him to articulate his theory of the Oedipus complex.[42]

Douglas, also dialoguing with Freud, deploys this openness of fiction and exploits it to the hilt. But instead of making an alternative world that we might believe in, he 're-combines' elements, so that the work offers a multitude of possibilities, not to believe in – you cannot believe in so many – but to actively engage, select, reject, amend, or endorse. His most famous experiment in this area is his 1998 video installation *Win, Place or Show*. This work can be seen in retrospective dialogue with *Dice, 1950*. The title of the installation invokes the issue of chance and risk again, in its reference to horse betting. As in *Der Sandmann*, the screen is split in the middle – but here more emphatically and materially – for no other necessity, it seems, than to reconfigure the split subjectivity Lacan theorised and Beckett staged. The two men in the scene are temporarily sharing a one-person flat. They represent typical white working-class males of the 1960s. The action scenes include discussions about conspiracy theory and the chances of betting wins, and conclude – if that word can be used in a looped re-combination work – with a fight between the two men.[43]

In *Dice, 1950* (p.27) the three men are harmoniously working together, in a space that the door behind them shows also to be confiningly shallow and small while their hats suggest they don't belong there, to 'place' and 'win'. Mates in crime, they belong to the *noir* ambience invoked also in *Cache, 1948* (p.31) and brought to a provisional but dubious narrative end in *Suspect, 1950* (p.25). There, the suspect is alone, without his mates, although the two supposed policemen

**42.** See Sigmund Freud, *Totem and Taboo*, trans. James Strachey, Routledge & Kegan Paul, London, 1950. The project Michelle Williams Gamaker and I have done is called on the whole *Mère Folle*, after the title of the 1998 book by Françoise Davoine that was the basis of our film, recently published in English as *Mother Folly*, trans. Judith H. Miller, Stanford University Press, Stanford, 2014. The feature film is called *A Long History of Madness*. See www.crazymother movie.com for the project, including the films, and www.miekebal.org/ exhibitions for descriptions and images of the installation works.

**43.** In a Lacanian reading of *Win, Place or Show* accompanied by a suggestive selection of stills, Gordon Lebredt offers a number of perspectives on the vertical seam, among which the 'nothing which the subject is', a literal vanishing point of the subject, an absence or stain, and more. See 'Living the Drive', *Parachute 103*, nos 7–9, 2001: pp.32–33. For an illuminating analysis of Douglas's most important works up to 2006, see Philip Monk, 'Discordant Absences', in *Stan Douglas* (ed.), Dumont Verlag, Cologne, 2006, pp.9–156. Intimacy in its intricate relationship to (intermale) violence – a prominent preoccupation in *Win, Place or Show* – is an extremely important issue in gender theory. See, for example, Ernst Van Alphen, 'The Homosocial Gaze According to Ian McEwan's *The Comfort of Strangers*', in *Art in Mind: How Contemporary Images Shape Thought*, University of Chicago Press, Chicago, IL, 2005.

who bring him in wear the hats the criminals donned in *Dice, 1950*. Cops? Then crooked. The categories don't work.

In *Win, Place or Show* the acted scene is repeated in a loop on two screens, slightly inclined, set up next to each other with a small gap between them, but the actors' positions in relation to the space and each other constantly shift from loop to loop. This would require a playing time of some 20,000 hours, before any one combination of images was repeated. This is fiction at its most critical; a fiction impossible to endorse, yet powerfully possible, if only we give chance a chance, so to speak.

It is possible to consider such re-combinatory devices not only as machines to produce fictional narratives, but also directions for use for other works. For this we only have to retain chance and multiplicity as features of Douglassian fiction. Why not consider the photograph *Burlap, 1948* (p.134) in such terms, for example? This is not a very plausible mode of reading an image that, to all intents and purposes, one would more easily give a social documentary frame of reference. A heap of burlap is lying on a wooden floor and against a wooden wall. That is all. But avoiding that social-documentary reading with its predictably indicting outcome is precisely the point of a fiction that reconfigures it. The precedent archival images bear a disambiguating caption, relating the image to those rendered famous by Luc Sante's 1992 book *Evidence*. But if such direct lineage was the point, Douglas could surely have made that reference clear? The title *Burlap* opens the image up to re-combining fictionalization.[44]

With the help of *Win, Place or Show*, we can see the piece of cloth on a dirty floor is random. It signifies strictly nothing – that is, unless we put ourselves in the narrative mode, suspending the disbelief that would require us to 'find out' what the image 'represents'. Then, the three elements – the worn wooden wall, the dirty floor, and the indifferent burlap object – lose their obvious coherence in a certain urban look, and can begin to produce narratives, all equally remote from reality. One can activate the baroque mode of looking and make the most of the curves, folds and waves in the burlap; consider its three-dimensionality, its volume and surface indistinct; its brightness compared to its surroundings; its non-figurativity, which affiliates it with *Intrigue, 1948* (p.29). More likely, though, one thinks there is a hidden body beneath it, a dead or sick victim of social inequity. Someone locked out; or someone locked in? What happened, and how does that lone corpse,

44. Luc Sante, *Evidence*, Farrar, Strauss and Giroux, New York, 1992. This book contains images of crime scenes from the years 1914 and 1918.

if it is one, end up so neatly hidden under that agonizingly ambiguous heap? We will never know.

Compared to *Burlap, Incident, 1949* (p.46) gives away much more to help us recombine available narrative elements. The use of newspaper to keep warm is known from life on the street – then and now. The busy print distracts almost but not quite from the two feet visible at the front that do reveal a person beneath it. The head sticking out from the stairwell is out of place. Someone so neatly coiffed and dressed simply does not belong in a shabby apartment building where homeless people sleep or lie dead on the landing. But the fictionality machine really gets going once we try to read his bent-over face. It is impossible to strictly determine whether the man is reading the paper, finding out what the day's incidents have been, or observing the incongruous spectacle in front of him, that constitutes in itself an incident. In this work from *Midcentury Studio,* otherwise so full of hands, there is no hand that lifts the paper.

Together, these two photographs, one strictly unreadable, the other barely, and ambiguously so, point to the unrealness of what we see. They proclaim an impossibility to 'believe' and hence, the need to suspend our disbelief. But the unrealness is constructed in such a way that the recombination of possible meanings, following the lead of Douglas's special brand of fictionality, does not *burden* us with a responsibility, as a moralizing ideology critique would, but compels us to *endorse* it. Maria Muhle has suggested that fiction was an alternative to the disabused realization that photography did not fulfil its promises of capturing reality:
'… the gradual fictionalization of reality as the means to *better* represent reality derives from the gradual loss of confidence in the photographic medium and its mimetic capacities, and this becomes apparent in the images in their ever more staged reality'.[45]

Muhle suggests the images achieve a kind of abstraction. And if we take abstraction in the sense in which Deleuze has developed that concept, the notion comes close to Douglassian fictionality. This opening up, in Douglas's re-combinations, is not limited to form but combines form and meaning in ever-changing ways to produce new possibilities of both. Instead of passively absorbing the meaning of the image closest to what we know – or think we know – the images compel us to suspend the need to recognize, to decide, and to believe. What Douglas proposes instead has been with us all along.[46]

45. Maria Muhle, 'The Magical Realism of Post-war America,' in O'Brian, op. cit., pp.54–55.

46. Ibid, p.57.

Buddy Black, Mary Jackson and Henry/Hank Williams

'Members of the jury, suspend your disbelief,' says the villain of *Helen Lawrence,* Walker/Wallace, when the manager of the hotel, Harry, is getting a little too close to unmasking him as the killer of Helen's husband. With these words he tries to dismiss as fiction the truth creeping in, but not without invoking the juridical situation in which such an opposition is a matter of life and death. After one of those quick repartees (Walker: I faint at the sight of blood; Harry: But you melt at the smell of pussy), and Harry's explanation of how he thought the murder had been committed, Walker proceeds to murder Harry in exactly that way.

Douglas does not aim to decide between truth and fiction here. It is the villain who says this, after all. Invoking the trial he would face if Harry went to court with this, killing the man is Walker's way of confessing. At this moment, first we see the projection of Harry's face as he fights for his life. Then, once he falls into the passivity of death (leaving Julie/Joe an orphan for the second time) a close-up of Walker's face betrays a multitude of emotions, from panic and fear to relief, despair over the new problem he is facing now, and astonishment about his own capability of killing – I am just speculating, reading what I could from the projected images. Instead of opposing fiction to truth, then, the work opposes a single fiction to a multitude. All this as part of the fiction that binds research, history and narrative to create the possibility for viewers to transgress temporal boundaries and access the past, not as historical truth to be captured, but to feel how history hold us in its grip.

## Hauntologist

Who, then, is Stan Douglas, as a subject who doesn't believe in subjectivity but makes art so strong that *its* subjectivity affects me so deeply? Perhaps this subject is a scrim of sorts. Accumulating its many functions in the play, the scrim of *Helen Lawrence* ends up as the interface between times, modes, and truth-value. In addition to everything mentioned so far, it now becomes crucial to see, recognise, and acknowledge the importance of the status of the scrim as *spectral*. With its varying transparency and opacity, before we know it,

47. Guy Debord, *The Society of the Spectacle,* Black & Red, Detroit, MI, 1992, 1967. Francis Bacon famously insisted his paintings should be shown behind glass to make seeing them more difficult, and thus enticing viewers to look better. See for his and other aspects of Bacon's work that, perhaps unexpectedly, relate to Douglas's, Ernst van Alphen, *Francis Bacon and the Loss of Self,* Reaktion Books, London, 1992 and 'Skin, Body, Self: The Question of the Abject in the Work of Francis Bacon', in Rina Arya and Nicholas Chare (eds), *Abject Visions: Powers of Horror in Art and Visual Culture,* Manchester

we will have been immersed, for an hour and a half, in a spectral vision, rather than a spectacle. Avoiding the kind of spectacle Debord so abhorred by making seeing more difficult and hence, more intense and engaged, is one of the many functions of the scrim. This is just as adequate a characterisation of Douglas's art.[47]

The aspects of research, history, narrativity and culminating in fictionality join forces in the idea, inspired by the phantom ride, of hauntology. Phantoms, ghosts, spectres – they don't exist, they are fictional – or are they? The precedent is a kind of ghost, but this only complicates the very idea of precedents; for precedents have their own precedents. Yet, in my view, Douglas's precedents provisionally halt that vertiginous *mise en abyme* at the beginning of the twentieth century, or the end of the nineteenth; his ghost is not primarily midcentury, but begins already at the completion of colonization, the closing of the frontier, and the start of cinema. The middle of the twentieth century is one such moment in which these ghosts irrepressibly return. It is the moment of decolonization – another unfinished project or failed utopia.

The phantom ride guides us, through the risky Rockies, to a place where we have been all along but now return with a mood for recombination: the world around us, with its haunting 'past imperfect' – a world that will never be simple again. Through his dense, heterochronic history, his looping or otherwise disturbed narrativity, always unfinished, and his fictions that activate rather than dull their viewers, the artist calls up what has become known, since Jacques Derrida's *Specters of Marx*, as 'hauntology'. For Derrida, the 'spectre of Marx' is the spectre of ongoing injustice Marx saw; and the French philosopher notes that since Marx's opening of *Das Kapital*, that spectre of injustice in the world has only gotten worse. This is his kick-off for the development of a 'philosophy of responsibility'. But what does such a philosophy of spectrality look like, and how can it be culturally implemented, without the heaviness, abstraction (in the negative sense of not-figuration), and limited access of philosophical discourse itself? Douglas the artist who is also a researcher experiments with this question.[48]

This brings us back to the phantom ride of Douglas's early work *Overture* (p.94). There is now much more to say about the

University Press, Manchester, 2015.

48. See Jacques Derrida, *Specters of Marx: The State of the Debt, the Work of Mourning, and the New International*, trans. Peggy Kamuf, Routledge, New York and London, 1993. Esther Peeren offers a brilliant demonstration of the real social relevance of the fictional imaginary of the spectre: *The Spectral Metaphor: Living Ghosts and the Agency of Invisibility*, Palgrave Macmillan, London, 2014. With Douglas, she rejects the opposition between fiction and reality and instead, shows the reality of fiction.

Chief James Muldoon

implications of this contemporary engagement with the early wonderment of spectators before such images. In a commentary on Tom Gunning's famous concept of 'cinema of attraction,' Verhoeff brings forward a crucial yet simple distinction in her attempt to distinguish films of this kind into more subtle categories:

> Both train and chase films rely on a primary narrative format of spatial mobility, but in a different way. The phantom ride shows this in a *first-person perspective* from a moving vehicle; the chase film 'follows' characters traversing space. These generic formats show different perspectives on the experience of mobility: one that invites a primary identification, and one that binds the mobility to a third person. Both solicit a heteropathic immersion based on spectatorial transportation via the visual mobility on the screen.[49]

The point of the invocation of the spectre is to allow, or encourage, the perspective Verhoeff calls a first-person perspective to be bound to the spectre, the phantom, or the ghost without erasing the ghost's otherness – the other, especially in a temporal sense. The spectre compels us to commit to a bond of the subject with the 'past imperfect'. The figure of the ghost is a trace of what was but is no more, yet cannot be excised from the present. But it can be endorsed as a point of identification in Verhoeff's sense, only with a subject as an 'unnamable last person' *à la* Beckett. This would be available for 'inhabiting a situation,' to recycle Douglas's phrase. This, then, allows the production of a subjectivity that is radically different from the self-centred subject of another kind of modernism.

It is easy to see in Douglas's oeuvre a significant number of spectral images. There are the double-layered images with their semi-transparency of *Suspiria* (2003), the ghost town of *Le Détroit* (1999), and many others where the trace supersedes reality, where decay is stronger than the present, and ghosts haunt the screen. One spectral recombinatory work is *Inconsolable Memories* (2005), an integration of film in 16mm on two 'recombined' reels, and photographies. This journey to Cuba-then recombined with Cuba-now is based on Tomás Gutiérrez Alea's 1968 film *Memorias del subdesarrollo* (Memories of Underdevelopment). In an article on this work, Lisa Coultard speaks of 'the hauntings and traces of lost potential, past encounters and missed futures'. She hits the nail on the head with her choice of words; this could as well be a characterisation of *Helen Lawrence*.[50]

The spectre comes from the past to ensure the past, imperfect as it is, remains inside the present, in order for a future to be possible, on the condition that it connects to the right spectre from the past. The spectre shows this possibility, dim as it is, like those moments when the scrim is more or less obscuring the stage but foregrounding the historicised close-ups of real faces, more real than the real ones on stage. This is indeed especially relevant in *Memorias del subdessarrollo*, this work on, and set in, Cuba. How can you *inhabit* a place that no longer exists, and the future of which has failed to come about, so that only ghosts of it wander around? This is the ongoing search in Douglas's work, and *Helen Lawrence* its most radical staging of this impossibility.

In *Midcentury Studio*, there are also images that suggest what Coultard calls 'the hauntings and traces of lost potential'. The spectres take different shapes, but all suggest a present where time has thickened and experience just may be heterochronous. One example is *Cricket Pitch, 1951*, a strong trace of empire. The entire sport of cricket is a ghost of the empire; this applies as much to the geography of it as to the players. In *Demobilization Suit, 1945* (p.42), the ghost seems particularly literal and destructive, with white paint functioning like orange flames, surrounding the man with a fire that erases his face and body. In *Trick or Treat, 1945* (p.146), the boys are masked, like the clown, and like Betty/Helen. The return of inequity is hinted at in the mask of the taller white man-boy, which casts what we call a dirty look, a furtive look of greed, to the bag of treats of the other kid. The two boys are not to blame for this effect on at least this viewer. But that absence of grounds for moralism does not make the spectral hint of greed and its disastrous consequences any less ominous. The heterochronic density is especially poignant as these are most likely to be children. From within the child's disempowerment they look to the future, but they are already haunted by the past. All these images compel 'inconsolable memories' – memories mourning what could have become; symmetrical to *Helen Lawrence* where all the characters seem to be mourning a future they cannot shape in the moment of losing what they (thought they) had.

Inhabiting a situation enables the experience of the temporality I have called heterochrony. At some moments in our interaction with Douglas's work, this inhabiting of a time of which only the ghost, phantom, or spectre continues to haunt us, the phantom ride of risk and danger can take us to a time – thick, heterogeneous, and full of promise – with which a 'first-person identification' is possible. From within such times, it is possible to take responsibility.

49. Verhoeff, 2012, op. cit., p.67.

50. Lisa Coultard, 'Reiterative Revolution', *Fillip* 3, Summer, 2006, accessed 15 March 2012: http://fillip.ca/content/reiterative-revolution.

For such voyages, a guide like Stan Douglas's videos and photographs, and now his filmed play or play-as-film *Helen Lawrence* can be a lead-in to a different vision. One small hint at this possibility framed by hauntology may be the fact that during the final, most irrational killing, when the drunk police officer Perkins accidentally kills the war veteran Henry, a shocked Buddy says: 'you killed my brother'. The policeman drenched in alcohol and corrupt habits can't find anything more apt to say then: 'Don't worry, we'll work something out. Alright, anybody see what happened? Anything? Anybody?' At that moment, Buddy, approaching him from behind, kills him with a blackjack. Is Buddy the spectre, coming up and hitting from behind, or is Perkins, whose drunken talk can only reiterate his abusive corruption?

The scrim turns transparent. All we see is the stage. And on it, behind Buddy, we see that strongest form of index: a large shadow. The shadow of Henry's traumatized past, of Buddy's long-term trauma as a black man living under the threat and mercy of the corrupt chief of police like so many; the shadow of this recent war, the wars long past but still haunting the present, including the Civil War, and of the wars of the future: so many shadows, even the aesthetic of *film noir* cannot be maintained. Not in front, but threateningly, behind the figure, the shadow is the spectre that we cannot prevent from following us. But nor can the subject see it. It is always behind, looming over it, larger than life, in the spatial variant of the past. Thus staged, time affects us, and then we do with it what we can and wish to do. The artist proposes, the viewer disposes.

opposite: *Midcentury Studio: Trick or Treat, 1945*, 2010
Digital fibre print mounted on Dibond aluminium
151.1 x 121.9 x 5.1 cm

*Corrupt File: 2013_9009*, 2013
Colour inkjet mounted on Dibond aluminium
200 x 156.2 x 7 cm

*Corrupt File: 2012_0279*, 2013
Colour inkjet mounted on Dibond aluminium
200 x 156.2 x 7 cm

*Corrupt File: 2012_0290*, 2013 (detail)
Colour inkjet mounted on Dibond aluminium
200 x 156.2 x 7 cm

# Acknowledgements

All works courtesy the artist, David Zwirner,
New York/London, and Victoria Miro, London
All dimensions given are as framed.

*Der Sandmann*, 1995
Two channel, 16mm film
installation, black and white,
sound, 9:50 mins (loop)

*Vidéo*, 2007
High definition video
installation, colour, sound
(six musical variations),
18:11 mins (loop)

*Midcentury Studio*:
Digital fibre print mounted
on Dibond aluminium

    *Clown, 1946*, 2010
    151.1 x 121.9 x 5.1 cm

    *Cache, 1948*, 2010
    75.2 x 86.7 x 4.4 cm

    *Intrigue, 1948*, 2010
    75.2 x 69.5 x 4.4 cm

    *Dice, 1950*, 2010
    187 x 150.8 x 7 cm

    *Suspect, 1950*, 2010
    74.6 x 87.9 x 4.4 cm

*Malabar People*:
Digital fibre print mounted
on Dibond aluminium

    *Cab Driver, 1951*, 2011
    104.1 x 78.7 x 5.1 cm

    *Dancer, 1951*, 2011
    104.1 x 78.7 x 5.1 cm

    *Female Impersonator, 1951*,
    2011
    104.1 x 78.7 x 5.1 cm

    *Longshoreman, 1951*, 2011
    104.1 x 78.7 x 5.1 cm

    *Owner/Bartender, 1951*,
    2011
    104.1 x 78.7 x 5.1 cm

    *Student, 1951*, 2011
    104.1 x 78.7 x 5.1 cm

    *Waitress I, 1951*, 2011
    104.1 x 78.7 x 5.1 cm

    *West-Side Lady, 1951*, 2011
    104.1 x 78.7 x 5.1 cm

*Corrupt File*:
Colour inkjet print mounted
on Dibond aluminium

    *2012_0157*, 2013
    200 x 156.2 x 7 cm

    *2012_0192*, 2013
    200 x 156.2 x 7 cm

    *2010_2329*, 2013
    200 x 156.2 x 7 cm

    *2012_0279*, 2013
    200 x 156.2 x 7 cm

    *2012_0290*, 2013
    200 x 156.2 x 7 cm

    *2010_3024*, 2013
    200 x 156.2 x 7 cm

*Hogan's Alley*, 2014
Digital C-print mounted
on Dibond aluminium
157.5 x 309.9 x 7.6 cm

*The Second Hotel
Vancouver*, 2014
Digital C-print mounted
on Dibond aluminium
305 x 157 x 7 cm

List of works

**Stan Douglas**
7 November 2014 – 15 February 2015
The Fruitmarket Gallery, Edinburgh

This book is published on the occasion
of the exhibition **Stan Douglas**
7 November 2014 – 15 February 2015
The Fruitmarket Gallery, Edinburgh

**Published by The Fruitmarket Gallery**
45 Market Street, Edinburgh, EH1 1DF
Tel: +44 (0)131 225 2383
info@fruitmarket.co.uk
www.fruitmarket.co.uk

Publication supported by
**David Zwirner**
519, 525 & 533 West 19th Street
New York, NY 10011
Tel: +1 212 727 2070

537 West 20th Street
New York, NY 10011
Tel: +1 212 517 8677
www.davidzwirner.com

**Victoria Miro**
16 Wharf Road
London N1 7RW
Tel: +44 (0)20 7336 8109

14 St George Street
London W1S 1FE
Tel: +44 (0)20 7205 8910
www.victoria-miro.com

Edited by Fiona Bradley
Designed and typeset by Elizabeth McLean

ISBN 978-1-908612-31-1

Distributed by Art Data
12 Bell Industrial Estate
50 Cunnington Street
London, W4 5HB
Tel: +44 (0)20 8747 1061
www.artdata.co.uk

cover: *Hogan's Alley,* 2014 (detail)
endpapers: production photographs from
**Helen Lawrence,** 2014

All works reproduced courtesy the artist,
David Zwirner, New York/London and
Victoria Miro, London. © Stan Douglas.

*Helen Lawrence*
Production photographs by Stan Douglas, 2014.
A production of Arts Club Theatre (Vancouver),
Banff Centre (Banff), Canadian Stage (Toronto)
and Stan Douglas Inc.
*Cast list:* Mary Jackson: Crystal Balint
Sergeant Leonard Perkins: Greg Ellwand
Chief James Muldoon: Ryan Hollyman
Henry/Hank Williams: Sterling Jarvis
Percy Walker/Wallace: Nicholas Lea
Buddy Black: Allan Louis
Eva Banks: Ava Jane Markus
Harry Mitchell: Hrothgar Mathews
Julie/Joe Winters: Haley McGee
Rose George: Mayko Nguyen
Betty Mansfield/Helen Lawrence: Lisa Ryder
Edward Banks: Adam Kenneth Wilson

Picture credits:
pp.14, 17–18, 21: installation views of *Der
Sandmann*, 1995, in 'The Oldest Possible
Memory: Sammlung 1', Sammlung Hauser &
Wirth, Lokremise St.Gallen, 2000. Photographs:
Stefan Altenburger Photography Zürich. p.33:
Anonymous, *Mine Town Blaze*, 1960, Private
collection, London. p.35: Anonymous, *X Marks
the Spot: Chicago Gang Wars in Pictures*, The Spot
Publishing Co. USA, 1930, p.41. p.37: ©
Luciano Rigolini, *What you see*, 2008 Collection
of Fotostiftung Schweiz Winterthur by
permission of the artist. p.38: © Henry Wessel,
*Incident No. 5*, 2013. Courtesy Pace/MacGill
Gallery, New York. p.41: © Cindy Sherman,
*Untitled Film Still #48*, 1979. Courtesy the
artist and Metro Pictures, New York. p.114:

© Henri Cartier-Bresson, *Natcho Aguirre, Santa Clara, Mexico,* 1934 © Henri Cartier-Bresson/Magnum Photos.

The Fruitmarket Gallery is a company limited by guarantee, registered in Scotland No. 87888 and registered as a Scottish Charity No. SC 005576. VAT No. 398 2504 21. Registered Office: 45 Market Street., Edinburgh, EH1 1DF

The Fruitmarket Gallery brings to Scotland the work of some of the world's most important contemporary artists.

We recognise that art can change lives and we offer an intimate encounter with art for free. We make exhibitions, commissions and publications directly in collaboration with artists.

We celebrate new thinking, and offer an international platform for artists, curators and writers, whether they have made their reputation here or abroad.

The Fruitmarket Gallery welcomes all audiences. We make it easy for everyone to engage with art, encouraging questions and supporting debate.

Publishing is an intrinsic part of The Fruitmarket Gallery's creative programme, with books published to accompany each exhibition. Books are conceived as part of the exhibition-making process, extending the reach and life of each exhibition and offering artists and curators a second space to present their work.